HEART
AND
SOUL

HEART ❧ AND ❧ SOUL

MELISSA BELL
WITH ANDREW CROFTS

JOHN BLAKE

Published by John Blake Publishing Ltd,
3 Bramber Court, 2 Bramber Road,
London W14 9PB, England

www.johnblakepublishing.co.uk

First published in hardback in 2010

ISBN: 978 1 84454 921 4

British Library Cataloguing-in-Publication Data:

A catalogue record for this book is available from the British Library.

Design by www.envydesign.co.uk

Printed in Great Britain by CPI William Clowes, Beccles, NR34 7TL

1 3 5 7 9 10 8 6 4 2

© Text copyright Melissa Bell/Andrew Crofts 2010

Papers used by John Blake Publishing are natural, recyclable products made
from wood grown in sustainable forests. The manufacturing processes
conform to the environmental regulations of the country of origin.

Every attempt has been made to contact the relevant copyright-holders,
but some were unobtainable. We would be grateful if the
appropriate people could contact us.

CONTENTS

PROLOGUE

The release of Alex's album at the end of 2009 resulted in a lot of stories appearing in the press about our family. I have chosen not to talk about some of these things when writing this book because I did not want to invade the privacy of my children or their father.

Although I have described my struggles as a single mother bringing up four children on my own, I did not think it was my place to go into detail about my ex-husband's love life, and I certainly wasn't going to talk about the love lives of my children.

It is true, as the newspapers have now revealed, that one of the girls with whom my ex-husband had an affair was underage at the time she allegedly fell pregnant by him, and that he served a prison sentence as a result.

I have never lied to the children about anything that happened between their father and me, but when they were small there seemed no reason why the rest of the world should know about our private business. I understand that now Alex is becoming famous it is pointless to hope that other people won't be tempted to come forward and talk about things that have happened which we might have preferred to keep to ourselves. It was a very painful period of our lives, but we have moved on successfully and I fully understand that the other women and children in his life have an equal right to speak up about the ways in which he has treated them.

There have also been a lot of press stories about Alex and me falling out. It is a fact that we both have strong opinions and we both have a tendency to speak our minds when perhaps we should be a little more diplomatic, and it is true that our quick tempers often lead to fireworks between us. In fact, most of the family is just as outspoken and volatile. But virtually every woman I know who has daughters in their teens and early twenties experiences a lot of highs and lows in their relationships; it is all part of family life, all part of growing up. I'm sure there were times when I gave my mother just as much reason to worry as my children give me.

This is the story of a normal, loud, loving family who have been put under abnormal pressure, firstly through the behaviour of my ex-husband and secondly because of the pressures of the modern star-making media. I'm not complaining about it because show business is the world I chose, always knowing that success would come at a price.

I am so proud of the way I and my children have remained a family unit through everything, and I'm sure there will be plenty more dramas before we are finished. They are, after all, the stuff of life.

⟨ CHAPTER ONE ⟩

STAYIN' ALIVE

Sitting in a bed for four or five hours every couple of days, having the blood slowly and methodically sucked out of my body by a machine, cleansed of all the poisons that have built up and then pumped back in, gives me a lot of time to think. It gives me a chance to remember the dreams I started out with in life and the amazing places that they have led me to.

Everyone starts out with dreams, hopes and ambitions, but they don't always work out quite how you expect. I guess it's like John Lennon once said, 'Life is what happens to you while you're busy making other plans.'

There's lots of other stuff to think about too. Not just the dark, dramatic, frightening chain of events that have come about inside my body and my DNA, leading to my being here in this bed, surrounded by machinery and screens, but the fabulous moments as well, like when I was standing on a stage singing strong and proud to millions of people around the world, or when I first heard my voice coming back to me off a little piece of black vinyl or out of my mother's bedside radio. I think about the future a lot too, and everything exciting that it holds for my family. If there wasn't so much to look forward to, perhaps it would be harder to get through the bad days, harder to make the effort needed to keep on living.

Today I'm going to be stuck in this bed for the full five hours because I was a little naughty yesterday and ate two nectarines. I knew I shouldn't be doing it, even as I was slipping them in between my lips and enjoying their taste and the soothing juice as it slid down my throat. In my heart, I knew that they would try to poison me, but the first one looked so tiny and innocent I told myself it couldn't possibly do me that much harm. And when I actually bit on it, it was so soft and so sweet and delicious the memory wouldn't go away and I just couldn't resist the temptation of having another one a few minutes later.

Even after all I have been through, I still wasn't able to stop myself and the moment I'd finished them I knew I was going to have to pay the price today. When I arrived on the ward this morning, I had to own up to the nurses and ask them to make sure that the potassium which I knew the succulent little fruits had deposited in my blood was all safely removed by the machine; otherwise, if it stays there, it will stop my heart from beating. My whole life now has to be about resisting temptations from all the seemingly innocuous everyday things that are trying to kill me, like they killed my mother and my grandmother before me, and maybe many other women in my family over the centuries.

Three days a week, I have to go through the same tedious

ritual, often lying in exactly the same hospital bed, with my hair scraped up inside an unflattering plastic cap. If I stopped coming for these sessions on the machine, I would almost certainly be dead within a week. You can't live without your kidneys – if your kidneys fail, you have to have dialysis to cleanse the blood and perform the function your kidneys usually would. The machine that stands beside the bed is my best friend and I have to remind myself of that whenever I am tempted to hate it. It is only because of that machine that I am here and able to enjoy the excitement of watching all our family dreams come true.

Some people decide that the pressure and worry of dialysis, coupled with the frequent exhaustion and other symptoms of kidney failure, is all too much and they deliberately give up coming to the clinic to be hooked up to the machines. They literally 'sign off' from the treatment, knowing that by doing so they are choosing to end their lives the moment they scribble their signature on the hospital form. I suppose it isn't exactly the same as committing suicide, more a question of 'letting nature take its course', but the result is still the same. It ends all hope of things ever getting better.

Kidney failure is not a painful death apparently, apart maybe from the terrible itching you get under the skin every time you eat anything, but the doctors can give you drugs to relieve that. Without the support of your kidneys, your body simply closes down. But I still don't understand what brings people to make that decision. I would never want to do that, never want to end my life deliberately just to avoid these sessions. It may be boring and an inconvenience to have to lie here for hours on end, but

3

surely it's better than dying. When I think back to the wonderful, overwhelming highs that I have experienced in my life, I wouldn't want to risk the chance of missing out on any more that the next few years might hold in store for me. Life has always been a struggle, but I believe the rewards are more than worth the fight.

There is so much I want to live for. I've produced four beautiful children and brought them up on my own and I want to see how they turn out. Our lives are too exciting and too full of possibilities for me to even consider giving up on it all now. I also like to flatter myself that they still need to have me around, at least some of the time.

Music was the first great love of my life and it has stayed faithful to me ever since I first discovered it. I can still put on earphones and listen to wonderful songs and I can still get up on a stage or go into a studio and sing whenever I'm asked, filling my lungs with air and loving the sounds that come out of my mouth. Music alone is reason enough to stay around on this earth as long as possible.

You can fit most things you want to do around dialysis sessions. I won't even let the need to be near a dialysis machine stop me travelling when I want to. I've learned that if you organise yourself carefully you can book in for sessions on a machine in most other countries, particularly in Europe, as long as you don't mind getting stuck into all the necessary paperwork. Basically all the authorities want to know is that you don't have HIV, which I don't, and after that it's just a question of emailing the right papers to the right people to make sure you have a bed reserved in a clinic somewhere at the moment you need it.

A few years ago, I was contacted on MySpace by an international soul band based in Germany, called T-MC, asking if I would sing with them. I went over to see them and we got on well. I recorded a song for their album and, as so often happens among people in the music business, they have gone on to become longstanding family friends. I'm going over there for the launch of the album next week. It will be my fourth visit and I've found a dialysis clinic I can go to for three mornings of treatment during my stay, which is right next to the hotel they've booked me into. I'll be able to walk round in my pyjamas if I want to. It would have been so easy to tell them that I couldn't go, that it was all too difficult, that I was too exhausted, but then I would miss a really great opportunity and, as long as I can still walk and breathe, laugh and sing, I want to enjoy every moment of my life to the full.

Officially I am still down on the records here in the hospital as 'Euphemia Burke', but everyone on the ward knows me as Melissa. Burke is my married name, so I prefer not to be called by it too often, even though it's the kids' name too. I love my kids more than anything and I wouldn't have wanted to miss the experience of bringing them into the world and watching them grow into beautiful, talented young adults, but if I could have managed it without marrying their father it would have saved us all a great deal of heartbreak. Being known by my husband's family name is an annoyance because that isn't really who I want to be and because he and his parents have been out of my life for so many years now. I prefer being called Melissa Bell.

I first became known as Melissa by accident when I was still at school. Some of the less nice kids kept chanting 'Euphemia's got Leukaemia' at me, so I started using my middle name, Imelda, instead. That led to my friends calling me Mel, and once other people had forgotten that I had ever been called Euphemia they just seemed to assume that 'Mel' was short for Melissa. I preferred it to Imelda so I didn't bother to correct them and before long it had become my name. That's how easily I became someone else.

The surname 'Bell', which I use most of the, time now was suggested by a friend of mine when I started singing professionally and needed something catchy to go with Melissa. That's how Melissa Bell came into existence, but Euphemia Burke still lives on in the records of the National Health Service and I never bother to correct the new nurses who think it is the best thing to call me. 'Euphemia' means 'to speak well' apparently, and comes from the Greek word for 'good'. St Euphemia was an early martyr who was burned at the stake. That's all very well, but to me it will always sound like 'leukaemia', with those childhood voices forever chanting in my memory.

So there are only two ways for any of us in this ward to come off these machines: one is to give up on life, which is not going to happen. The other is to have a kidney transplant, which means finding a match. That is never easy, and it is even harder when you have a blood group as rare as mine. I have the blood of so many different races coursing through my veins that there aren't too many people to match up with, and most of the ones who do exist live deep in the tropical mountains of Jamaica and aren't exactly clamouring to give up their body parts to some woman from a council estate in north London any time soon.

I'm not the only one with this problem by any means. Just one person in this ward has been able to have a transplant in the year since I started coming here, whereas I know of a couple who have simply given up hoping and have signed off to die.

The daily routine here is always the same. They hook us up to the machines on a 'first come, first served' basis, so I always want to be the first in the queue when they open the doors to the clinic at seven in the morning. I want to make sure that I will be the first to finish, when there is still at least half the day left for me to do something. It would be all too easy to surrender the whole day to the treatment and end up with no time for anything else at all. Over the last year I would have missed some of the greatest moments of my life if I had allowed the treatments to last all day.

Sometimes I don't even bother to get dressed before coming in, just climbing out of bed, pulling on some light pyjamas, running downstairs to the car and driving to St Pancras Hospital, desperate to get there before the ambulances arrive and start disgorging all the other patients they have picked up on their way in.

There are about a dozen beds and machines in the ward that I go to, and you get to recognise the same tired, familiar faces as they start to arrive each morning. Not many live as close to the hospital as I do, so I am nearly always there before anyone else. We all know one another well enough to nod 'hello' and 'goodbye' a few hours later, but for some reason people don't seem to want to talk while they're undergoing their treatment. It's as if they have entered their own internal worlds, lying on the beds, the machines patiently ticking and turning and beeping beside them. I would love to chat, just to help pass the hours, but I can see that others would not welcome it, so I keep myself to myself, just like everyone else. The upside of that is that it gives me all this time to think. Everything has happened in such a rush over the last few months and in a funny way it's helpful to have some quiet time to try to work it all out and get some perspective on all the excitement and glamour, all the emotions and the demands. Everyone benefits from taking a little time to stop and think now and again.

Digital displays on the machines tell me how much time I have left before the job is done, how much fluid my body still has to get rid of. I spend my time thinking, reading, dozing. I listen to my headphones. I usually like to have my radio tuned into LBC, a local London talk station. Music has been such a huge part of my life and for many years I hardly did anything else but listen to it and sing along to it, but now I find I like to learn about other things as well. I like to try to find out a bit about how the world around me works, to try to make a little sense out of what has happened to us.

My great love affair with music hasn't dimmed, but there is room in my head for other things now as well. I like reading biographies of successful people, many of them in show business or the recording industry – finding out how they achieved what they did, comparing their experiences with mine, imagining how I might be able to do the same as they did, either for myself or for my children. We have had some fantastic successes already, but that doesn't mean we couldn't be doing it better, couldn't climb higher and have even more great experiences.

Now and then the dialysis machine will clog up, or I will make too big a movement and it will react badly to the disturbance of the tubes, making me jump back to reality from wherever my mind has wandered, angrily bleeping at me to reset it, which I can do for myself now without always having to trouble the overworked nurses. I used to feel a surge of panic whenever one of the alarms went off, but I've grown used to them over the months. I know it is just part of the unpleasant routine.

They give me a drug to stop my blood from clotting during the process because apparently that can happen sometimes. It seems like nothing in my body can be relied on to do the job it's meant to do any more. The machines here are second-hand ones, donated to us by Barnet Hospital and refurbished. We are very grateful to have them. If only there had been more machines around 20 years ago, maybe my mother would not have had to die so early and so uncomfortably. She was a good woman and she didn't deserve any of what she had to go through. But I guess none of us does, and if you want your share of the lucky breaks you have to take the bad luck that comes along with them.

CHAPTER TWO

IVAN'S CHOICE

My mum and dad, Ivy and Ivan Ewen, arrived in England in 1958 on a Spanish boat called the *Begona*, which carried thousands of immigrants to Southampton from the West Indies with promises of jobs and glittering new lives in England, luring them away from the poverty of the islands. After the Second World War, it had taken hundreds more migrants from Europe down to new lives in Australia, and before that it was a troop ship going under the name of the *Vassar Victory*. It's hard to imagine in these days of casual air travel how many people were being ferried around the world by sea in the recent past, moving at an altogether statelier pace, many of them travelling in the hope of exchanging their old lives for something more exciting.

It was also the year that Elvis Presley was being drafted into the US army and the newly launched Cliff Richard was singing 'Move It', which John Lennon would later describe as the 'first English rock record'. It must have been an exciting time to be young and full of dreams for a better future.

In fact, in comparison with most of the West Indians who arrived on boats like the *Begona* and the better-known *Windrush*, my parents weren't really poor at all. Dad was already a successful entrepreneur with a string of dry-cleaning and pressing shops in Jamaica, but I think he believed he would be able to rise to even greater heights in England, making enough money in a few years to return home a truly wealthy man, able to build his own house and live a comfortable life. It has always been a tried and trusted way for ambitious young men to establish themselves, heading to places where the wages are going to be higher than in their homelands, where they believe it will be possible to build up a little nest egg for the future. Dad was a man of dreams and ambitions, although those dreams never seemed to quite work out as well as he hoped.

I still miss Dad terribly. Although he was a small man physically he was a larger-than-life personality – I wouldn't have been able to manage without him when the children were small and I was left to bring them up on my own. He would have been so proud to see what Alexandra has achieved, to hear her voice everywhere he went and to stand in places like London's O2 arena and see her up on stage, singing in the New Year in front of tens of thousands of cheering people, standing alongside Will Young, with Elton John banging away at the piano beside them.

We are a real melting pot of a family, like many people from the West Indies: the result of many centuries of trading, immigration, adventuring and slavery. Dad was half Jamaican and half Indian, Mum was half Jamaican and half Irish, so I guess it's not surprising that there aren't many people in the world who share my blood group. Dad was a handsome man, but tiny and skinny. He was no more than five feet tall, but he had a big voice to make up for it. He was trained as a tailor before he discovered he could make more money out of cleaning and pressing clothes rather than making them.

He was never work-shy, and as soon as he arrived in north London he took a job with a Cypriot family who owned the Alex Dry Cleaners chain. They had a few branches, one of which was next to the Rainbow Theatre in Finsbury Park, which was where Dad went to work. He still used his tailoring skills as well to earn a little extra, doing alterations for people, and making clothes too if they asked, mainly slacks. There was always a sewing machine standing in the corner of any room we lived in and people would come to him with patterns and lengths of material to get him to make clothes for them.

The Rainbow was something of a landmark in the area. It had originally been an Astoria cinema but in the 1960s the management started staging one-night concerts by the stars of the day. Everyone from Shirley Bassey to Ray Charles, Frank Sinatra to the Rolling Stones and Aretha Franklin to the Beatles appeared there. Many of the great events of modern musical history happened there. It was where Jimi Hendrix first set light to one of his guitars on stage and where David Bowie later staged his renowned 'Ziggy Stardust' concerts. It was converted into the Rainbow Theatre in 1971, relaunched with a concert by the Who, and became a world-famous venue where everyone from the Jacksons to Bob Marley came to play. Now the live acts have moved on to bigger concert halls, stadiums and arenas but the building is still there, looking much the same.

Many of the biggest stars who played at the Rainbow would bring their costumes next door to Alex Dry Cleaners and they would ask for Dad personally because they loved the care he took over his work, often showing their appreciation by giving him free tickets to get us into their shows. To my child's imagination, being given free tickets felt like we lived at the very heart of the show-business world, like we were personal friends of the stars who everyone else was having to pay hard-earned money to see.

Mum was a big, beautiful, buxom woman, who looked like Carmen Miranda with her coffee-coloured skin and thick, dark hair piled high. She had a beautiful singing voice but never thought of turning professional. She had worked in Jamaica as a hairdresser, which gave her a skill she could use to earn money once she arrived in London, and show business would have seemed a distant and inaccessible world to her. I wish she could have been around to see how far Alexandra has gone, how her granddaughter has benefited from the decisions and sacrifices she made all those years ago.

Both Mum and Dad had had children in previous marriages but I was the only child they had together who survived, and that made them incredibly protective of me. Frances was Dad's daughter, who lived with us and as a child always looked on Mum as her real mother. Frances's birth mother had handed her over to Dad as soon as she was born, saying she wanted nothing to do with the child. Dad took responsibility for her with the help of his sister, until he met and married Mum when Frances was two years old. Mum always treated the two of us the same, never showing any favouritism that I could see.

Dad was never married to Frances's real mum but both Frances and her birth mother are dead now, so there's no way of finding out the truth of what their relationship might have been like all those years ago, on those hot nights in Jamaica when Dad was probably as careless as most young men with only one thing on their minds.

Later, when she was grown up, Frances came to resent Mum, believing that she had split Dad up from her real mother, which was a shame because it seemed to me that they always had such a good relationship when Frances was young. The pressures of life so often drive wedges between family members as children grow up and begin to assert themselves.

Sonia was Mum's daughter from her first marriage to a local Chinese businessman. (There is a large Chinese community in Jamaica.) Mum told me that their marriage broke down after their first son, Danny, died from consumption when he was two and she didn't manage to conceive again. Mum continued to have problems conceiving again after meeting Dad and it was eight years after they were married before she finally found herself pregnant with me, which was, I think, another reason why they were both so protective of me. Having had so much trouble making me in the first place and having had to wait so long, they didn't want to run any risk of losing me.

By the time I was born, in 1964, a lot had been happening on the British music scene. *Top Of The Pops* had been going on the BBC since the beginning of the year and the Beatles were singing 'Can't Buy Me Love' and 'A Hard Day's Night'. Jamaican singer Millie Small, the daughter of a sugar-plantation overseer, whose stage name was simply Millie, had a quirky little hit with 'My Boy Lollipop' (the first major hit for Island Records after Chris Blackwell, the label's founder, discovered her and brought her to England in 1963), and Cilla Black was belting out 'You're My World' and 'Anyone Who Had a Heart'. Peter and Gordon had released 'World Without Love' (Millie had a brief relationship with Peter) and Billy J. Kramer was singing 'Little Children'.

I, on the other hand, was not 'little' or 'small' at all, weighing a massive 13lb (almost twice the average weight of a newborn baby), and my birth actually killed Mum. The hospital had even called in a priest to give her the last rites. Dad had already been brought to the hospital by the police, where the doctors told him that he was going to have to choose between saving his wife and saving his unborn baby so that they would know what to do in the operating theatre.

Although I know how much they had both wanted to have me, Dad had to make a choice and he told them that they should try to save my mother.

I guess he thought that he and Mum could always try again for another baby but that he would never be able to replace her. It must have been a horrible decision to be forced to make and I don't blame him at all for choosing Mum over me because he'd never met me, and I know how much he loved me once I arrived.

I had to be delivered by Caesarean section and, despite the surgeon's best efforts, Mum's heart stopped beating while she was still on the operating table. They called the priest into the theatre to administer the last rites and as he stood over her prone body on the operating table there was a miracle. Mum's heart started to beat again. At the same time as she was coming back to life, the midwife had managed to get me to take in a lungful of air and I let out a loud cry, the first musical note of my life. I'm sure it must have brought a great deal of joy to all those who heard it and who just a few minutes earlier had thought I would not live. Having thought for a moment that he was going to lose both of us, Dad found in an instant that he had his beloved wife back and a bouncing great baby girl with a powerful pair of lungs as a bonus.

That was also the year when the Supremes had their first worldwide hits with 'Where Did Our Love Go?', 'Baby Love' and 'Stop in the Name of Love', and changed everything for black female singers. A few years later, Diana Ross would go solo and become one of the biggest stars in the world, but I am getting ahead of myself.

Although her life had been spared, Mum's health never really recovered after that traumatic day – although perhaps she would have become ill anyway, regardless of whether I had come along when I did. She was already diabetic, which was the reason why I was such an enormous baby, feeding greedily on the sugar in her blood while I was inside her womb. Gestational diabetes is apparently very common among Jamaican women. (Insulin is a hormone and sometimes the other hormones of pregnancy block its usual action to make sure the baby gets enough glucose, creating a need for more insulin.)

Even once I was out of the womb, however, Mum and Dad's troubles with their new baby were not over. Three weeks after I was born, the doctors found a growth in my back. I was operated on immediately and it turned out to be benign, but I was still left with a scar down 80 per cent of my back. It has grown with me and is still there today as a reminder of just how precarious my entry into the world was, and how I nearly didn't make it. It seemed that right from the start I had been marked out as someone who was going to have to struggle to stay alive for her allotted span on earth. Watching their baby daughter being wheeled off into the operating theatre must have been like a nightmare to Mum and Dad, especially when they had just been through such a terrible trauma during the birth. And it was surely yet another reason why they were so protective of me while I was growing up, wanting to keep me away from every possible danger that they imagined might be lurking in the world outside our home, waiting to pounce. They knew already how easy it was to lose a small child.

But, however much we watch over our children, accidents will always happen and I believe that more come about inside the home than outside it. When I was four, we still didn't have an inside bathroom and so we used to fill an iron tub in front of the fire in the front room with boiling water from saucepans heated up on the stove. Mum was filling the tub one day and I became impatient with the whole laborious process, wanting to play in it immediately. Not realising that the water was still boiling hot, I plunged my arm in up to the shoulder while Mum was looking the other way. The skin all the way up my arm was burned, leaving yet more scars that are still with me today as a reminder of how easily accidents can happen. Despite having lived with the scars all these years, I don't remember the actual incident, but I do remember the subsequent ambulance ride to the hospital with Dad, the wailing of the sirens and the worried look on his face. Yet again they had seen how easily they could lose or damage me and their determination to keep me swathed in cotton wool grew stronger still.

They had both lost too much in their lives to be willing to allow me to take any unnecessary risks. Despite the restrictions which their fear put on me, it also made me feel very loved and very special at the same time.

⌒ CHAPTER THREE ⌒

SATURDAY NIGHT IS PARTY NIGHT

Arriving in the country with some money in his bank account, Dad was able to buy us a small house, which immediately turned into a busy, crowded, happy family home with a constant stream of friends and relatives coming and going. With two grown-up sisters and our grandmother, Icilda Russell, living with us, I was the only child among the adults and so I existed confidently at the centre of everyone's attention. But, even though I was spoiled in many ways, I was still never allowed out on my own to play like the other children in our street. I wasn't even allowed to cross the road from our house to school on my own. Even when Dad finally agreed to buy me a bike, which had taken a lot of nagging from me, he would insist on always walking along behind me when I went out, like a policeman on his beat, so I could never really experience the freedom that most children enjoy when they get their first wheels.

Yet I didn't really see it as a problem because in other

ways I was given everything I wanted and, maybe to compensate for my lack of freedom, Dad made food my friend. He was constantly lavishing sweets and takeaway food on me and always encouraging me to eat more. He would take me out to the local Wimpy Bar whenever I asked, allowing me to order two burgers at a time, or he would escort me down to the sweet shop and egg me on to fill my pockets with whatever I wanted. The first Wimpy Bar had opened in London in 1954, selling hamburgers in the Lyons Corner House in Coventry Street, between Piccadilly Circus and Leicester Square. The whole idea of fast food and hamburgers must have seemed as new and different and American to the British public as rock and roll itself. By the time I was six, Wimpy had a thousand branches around the world and it seemed to me like they must have been there for ever.

Not surprisingly, from being a sweet-looking toddler I developed into a seriously fat child but my weight was never the slightest concern to me. I was perfectly happy with my body, every last inch of it. I just loved to eat. I believe that, if Mum had understood more about the diabetes that was already starting to make her own life such a misery, she would have known that by allowing me to consume so much sugar when I was a child she was possibly making it inevitable that I would follow in her footsteps. People didn't talk about that sort of thing in those days. There wasn't any of the information which appears all over the media today about health and nutrition. Jamie Oliver, whose admirable mission would be to improve the nation's diet, hadn't even been born yet. We just ate the things that were cheap and available and tasted nice, which wasn't always the best idea, and then we'd have seconds.

Things went well for me at school. I was pretty advanced at reading and writing because my sister, Sonia, who was very educated and went on to attend university, had spent so much time helping me at home. My piano playing was also great for my age because of my grandmother's input. I was never short of people in the family who wanted to help me and teach me things and applaud whatever I did. Families are the most important things in the world. You can endure any amount of poverty and illness and difficulty if you are surrounded by people who love you and support you and who you know you can rely on to be there when you need them, even if they don't have any more money than you do. Without that unconditional support network, it must be very hard to survive in the world when things are going against you. In that respect, I was blessed from the day I was born and was allowed to survive through those first dramatic weeks.

Mum and Dad had chosen the house we were in because it stood directly opposite the school that they wanted me to go to, but I was still never allowed to walk across the road on my own: I had to be escorted back and forth by an adult at all times. It didn't bother me and I loved everything about school, always wanting to work hard and please the teachers. I must have impressed them because when the Queen came on an official visit there was a film crew there and I was asked to skip around the corridors and represent the school for their cameras. Our whole family was fantastically keen on the royal family and everything British, so I felt it was a huge honour to be chosen. For a long time after the film was shown on television, people would recognise me as the chubby little girl they had seen on their screens that night and I liked that attention – my first little moment in the spotlight. At that stage in my life, I would never have had the nerve to stand up in front of an audience and perform in public, but I was already developing a taste for winning the approval of audiences.

Although no one in the family gave it a second thought, the school doctors were becoming increasingly concerned about my weight and they actually went as far as placing me under medical supervision. That made no difference to my eating habits at all because Dad still said it was all right for me to eat two burgers at a sitting, followed by a bag of sweets. As long as he was offering, I was happy to accept whatever was dangled in front of me, and I hated the doctors for talking to Mum and me like we were idiots when we went to see them. Looking back now, I guess they thought my parents were ignorant and didn't understand the importance of nutrition, and I suppose they were right, because no one paid as much attention to their diet as they do now.

I noticed that in many ways our house seemed to be quite different from other West Indian homes that we visited. I actually think that sometimes Mum believed she was white, because she never gave me any idea that I was black or that our family was any different from any other British family. We ate very English meals most of the time and it came as quite a surprise to me when I finally realised that I was from an ethnic minority. It wasn't just me who was surprised either. All my white school friends, when they reached the age where they started to notice people's different skin tones, told me that they always thought of me as being 'just like them'. It's such a shame we can't all be as non-judgemental as children all our lives.

Every Saturday night, however, Mum and Dad would throw huge West Indian-style parties, with their Blaupunkt stereo blaring out and the house full of happy, laughing, drinking, dancing people, most of them Jamaican families who had arrived like them on the *Windrush* or the *Begona*. I would be desperate to stay downstairs for as long as possible, in the heart of the action, soaking up the music, but eventually I would be sent up to bed. There I would lie, listening to the joyous sounds bubbling up from below and wishing I could go back downstairs and join in again, but eventually I would fall asleep despite the thumping beats and raucous laughter. So much of the music of that period must have infiltrated my dreams on those Saturday nights, becoming part of my very soul as I slept.

I never had a room of my own in that house – there just wasn't enough space – so I would always be sharing a bed with my mother or my sister or my grandmother. I didn't care because I was used to it. I thought all families were like that, and it was a surprise to me when I eventually started to visit my friends' houses and discovered that they had their own bedrooms and their own beds. It looked incredibly luxurious to me for anyone to have so much space and privacy, let alone children.

So many of the people who used to come to those Saturday parties are still our family friends today, as well as their children and grandchildren. I remember Mr Buchanan, who used to work for Coca-Cola and brought some sample cans of Tango and Seven-Up to the house for me to taste before they were even launched on the market. I was so excited when the advertisements came out a few months later, knowing that I had tried them before anyone else, boasting about it to everyone at school for days afterwards. Mr Buchanan's daughter, Verna, became like another sister to me. She had come to England with him but her mum had stayed in Jamaica and so my mum took over the maternal role in England, something she was always very comfortable doing for the children of friends.

My grandmother used to give classical piano lessons in the house. By the time I was four, I could play pretty fluently and music filled every corner of my life even before I realised it. But once I'd discovered pop music all I wanted to do was listen to the radio and sing along to the hits of the day. I started running my own radio station out of the upstairs windows of the house. I would sit by an open window, waiting impatiently until someone came past and then I would shout out to them, begging them to stop and listen while I played them songs, doing introductions just like the disc jockeys I loved so much. Some of them would just laugh and walk on but others would stop and listen for a minute or two, indulging a little girl in her fantasies. I varied my broadcasts between the front window, which overlooked the street, and the back one, which looked out on to a factory where the workers would be coming or going at certain times of the day. I don't think Mum and Dad ever knew what was going on above their heads.

The seeds of my obsession with music had been sown and were already beginning to sprout, although I didn't yet have any idea in what direction it would take me. These days, I dare say, even four- and five-year-olds know about *The X Factor* and other talent shows, and dream of being discovered by Simon Cowell or Louis Walsh, or being mentored by Cheryl Cole or Dannii Minogue, but those were less knowing times for a child to be growing up in. Were we ignorant, or just more innocent? Maybe a bit of both.

CHAPTER FOUR

COLD, DARK MORNINGS IN ST PANCRAS

The clinic I go to is beside the railway lines, just behind St Pancras Station, one of the great historical sites of London and the location for films as varied as the Harry Potter films and the Spice Girls' first music video, for their hit 'Wannabe'. Each day, hundreds of workmen arrive there to continue the task of restoring the station to its former Victorian glories now that it has become the home of London's high-speed rail service to Europe. Their labours fill the air with dust and line the roadsides with screens and hoardings, masking the scale of the project as the rest of the city's life goes on all around them.

If the morning is cold and dark when I arrive at the clinic, I will invite the other patients to wait with me in my car until the staff open the doors and let us into the welcome warmth of the ward. As we sit there chatting, some of them tell me they're surprised to find that I drive myself to the clinic. Hardly any of the other patients drive any more, but, even if it is a struggle, I prefer to live a normal life whenever the exhaustion isn't too over-whelming. Besides, if I didn't have the car, I would find it very hard to get to all the places I want to get to in the few hours I have left each day. To me it seems that some people give up on life very easily.

A lot of us regulars in the ward are from Caribbean or Asian backgrounds. I don't know why that is – maybe it has something to do with our diets, or maybe it's a secret buried in our DNA, a ticking time bomb of chemicals waiting to go off and derail our lives from the moment we are born. But, of course, whatever their ethnic background, for wives, daughters, mothers and grandmothers, there is never a good time to be struck down like this.

It may be a bit of a generalisation, but I have found that people from the West Indies have a lot of funny habits and beliefs, some of which we carry with us wherever we go in the world. For a start, we don't like going to see the doctor to get things checked out, even when we are feeling terrible and could obviously do with some help. Maybe it's because we're stoical or somehow fatalistic about life. Or perhaps it's because we just don't want to hear bad news, preferring to stick our heads in the sand and keep on enjoying the moment for as long as we can before we eventually have to face up to the fact that we are mortal and sooner or later the party is going to have to end and the music is going to be switched off.

We don't like to be cut either, so we tend not to rush to donate our organs, believing we should go back to God at the end of our lives in the same state that he made us, with no cuts or incisions. I lost that battle when I was three weeks old and the surgeons sliced open my tiny little back to remove the suspicious-looking growth. If there was any chance of finding a new kidney, I would be more than happy to surrender to the scalpel again.

There are usually more men than women patients on the ward. In fact, at one stage, I was the only woman in here. Maybe that's why hardly anyone speaks to one another once we are in through the doors. In my experience, most men don't tend to like to communicate quite like we do, seeming to prefer to internalise everything. Having said that, I'll admit that the man who lucked out and had the kidney transplant used to like a bit of conversation to pass the time, but most don't. He was very educated and eloquent and I enjoyed talking to him, but once you've got a new kidney you never have to go on a dialysis machine again (unless that one packs up on you too), so I haven't seen him since.

Even though every bed in the ward is occupied, it can feel quite isolated sometimes, just lying there with the nurses bustling about their business around the beds and behind the screens, listening to the sound of the machines, waiting for it all to be over so I can get back in the car and go home to my own unmade bed. For those few hours, it feels like you have no control over your own life, no freedom of choice in what you do. Some people find it comforting to have other people making all their decisions for them. They become institutionalised and seem to lose the will to do anything else. I am determined not to let that happen to me.

Getting up early on these mornings is almost always

painful. When the alarm goes off at a quarter to six the last thing I want to do is drag myself out from under the covers and on to the streets of King's Cross. Even at that hour of the morning the traffic is already heavy because of all the building and development work that has been going on around the area, and because people are already starting to arrive for work in the new office blocks that have been opening up in previously neglected streets.

Before leaving the house, I have a quick wash, pull on whatever clothes I need that day, whether it is just pyjamas or a dressing gown, or something more formal if I might be going on somewhere after I've finished the treatment. I don't want to wear anything heavy because the first thing the staff do when they let us in is weigh us to find out how much fluid we have put on since we were last there and I don't want to make things seem any worse than they are.

I never pee any more. My kidneys have failed totally and all the poisons and bad stuff which they should be taking out of my blood and turning into urine just stay there until the machine extracts them, running round and round in my veins, waiting for a chance to kill me, hoping I'll get careless and allow them an opportunity to strike. It's shocking how much you miss something as simple as having to go to the toilet every few hours, something that you once took for granted or at most saw as a bit of a nuisance.

The ward is empty and waiting for us when the doors of the clinic are finally opened, the machines all cleaned out and disinfected, standing ready beside each bed for us to be hooked up. The nurses move quietly and briskly around them, making sure all our notes are in the right places and that we will have everything we need as we arrive. We look for our folders to see which bed we have been allocated, like guests at some formal dinner looking for our place names, or children searching for their names on school notice boards.

'Who's first?' someone carrying a clipboard asks.

'That's probably me,' I usually say, slightly embarrassed by my own keenness, but still determined not to lose my place in the queue and end up wasting more of the day than I need to. The others probably think I'm a bit pushy, always trying to be the first to be hooked up.

The tubes go into previously opened holes in my chest, one to carry the contaminated blood out, the other to bring the filtered and cleaned blood back in. It would be better if they could go into my arm, but the nurses haven't yet been able to find a vein there that's big enough to do the job. They keep searching and working at it. Once I'm connected up, the machine starts humming and a nurse brings me a little polystyrene cup of tea and a piece of toast to give me a bit of strength. I just sip at the tea because I don't want to use up my daily fluid allowance too quickly in case I want to drink something else a bit more delicious later in the day. Each day I'm only allowed three-quarters of a litre of fluid. That's the big problem about not peeing any more: you can't risk taking the fluid in if you have no way of letting it out. Imagine how frustrating it is not to be allowed to have a long drink of cold water when it's a hot day and you're really thirsty. At moments like that all I can do is suck on an ice cube.

I settle back to concentrate on my thoughts and my memories. My life has turned out to be very different from anything I ever expected.

CHAPTER FIVE

JAMAICAN NIGHTMARE

Things were going pretty well for Dad in those early days in London. He had been able to buy a house, and he had a steady job at the dry cleaner's, which he enjoyed, and lots of friends. He even bought himself a new car, a top-of-the-range Vauxhall limousine, or at least that was what it seemed like to me at the time. Not all the neighbours liked his flash ways, but I noticed they still liked to come to his Saturday-night parties. He eventually lost the car because he got drunk one evening and forgot to take the keys out of the ignition when he got home. (Believe it or not, it only became illegal to drink and drive in England in 1967, and I expect it was a while after that before men like Dad thought the law actually applied to them.) By morning, the car was gone, never to be seen again.

Next he got a really smart Hillman Hunter (a bit like a Ford Cortina), which was new on the market around that time. It had white bodywork and a black roof and it was his pride and joy.

Although Dad was earning quite well, Mum also contributed to the family budget by getting paid to look after friends' children. Most of them were women who had come from the West Indies like us and needed to work all week in order to support themselves and their families. The kids used to be delivered to our house on Monday mornings with mountains of nappies and food to see them through the week and Mum used to put them in any spare corner she could find. All our beds were always full of other people's children but nobody minded. It was like it was the normal way for people to live and Mum was just providing a service that the other women needed. I dare say nowadays some nosy neighbour would complain to social services and there would be people from the council coming round to inspect her. She would probably be closed down in no time, but then it all seemed perfectly normal and acceptable.

Mum also made extra money by doing her friends' hair for them at the weekends, styling their wigs on plastic heads so they could pull them on for parties on a Saturday night. These were the days when the musical *Hair* was playing on the London stage. It had starred the beautiful Marsha Hunt, who then went out with Mick Jagger and eventually had his baby. Her giant Afro hairstyle was famous and everyone was trying to emulate it, even the men. Jimi Hendrix had led the way in the late 1960s, of course, but then there had been movies like *Shaft* to carry it on and make 'big hair' acceptable for the man and woman in the street, not just the rock stars. The Afro became as much a part of 1970s fashion as flares and platform boots.

I liked the fact that the house was always full of people and voices and activity, and I also liked the biscuits that the children arrived with, surreptitiously slipping them into my own mouth whenever no one was looking.

Mum said I could have a cat of my own, and I ended up getting several over the years. They were all male for some reason, maybe because they were the ones people wanted to get rid of. I chose to ignore that fact and gave all of them female names like Linda, Mary-Jane and Katie because I was fixated with girls. I would draw pictures of girls all the time, making up names and life stories for them, colouring in their patchwork clothes. Patchwork was really fashionable at the time and I longed to have outfits of my own like that, but no one would buy them for me. I was living out a sort of fantasy life through my cats and my pictures.

'But this is a boy cat,' my sister would try to reason with me. 'He should have a boy's name.'

'No, I want to call her Mary Jane!' I was adamant, so my sister would just laugh and shrug and leave me to it.

Although we were living in a small house and I never had a bedroom of my own, Mum and Dad were both always working hard, which meant we were never without money for the necessities of life, so in the beginning I didn't realise we were hard up at all. I just thought we were normal.

In 1972, having been in England for 14 years, Dad must have felt that he had made enough money, because he decided to sell the house in London and return to his homeland to build the house he had always dreamed of and set himself up in business again. So the first time I saw Jamaica was when we returned that year, when I was eight, flown into Kingston Airport by BOAC, as British Airways then was.

This was the year when Michael Jackson was singing 'Ben' and 'Rockin' Robin', Sly and the Family Stone were singing 'Family Affair' and Roberta Flack had her first monster hit with 'The First Time Ever I Saw Your Face' after Clint Eastwood chose it for the soundtrack of his directorial debut *Play Misty for Me*.

My grandmother decided to stay in England and not to come with us. She rented a room from the Charles family, some friends of ours who had a house not far away in Tottenham. Even though we moved around a lot in the coming years, we were always renting from friends or staying with relatives; we were never in strangers' houses. No matter where we were or how cramped our living conditions became, we were always surrounded by familiar, friendly faces. It's the same in my house today, with people coming and going all the time, sharing rooms, sharing beds, sleeping on bunks and sofas and floors. People always need to have places to go where they will be among friends at difficult times of their lives when they are newly arrived in a city or between homes of their own for whatever reason. If families and friends don't open their doors to people when they need shelter, that is when the unlucky ones end up sleeping on the streets and sliding to the bottom of the pile. That sense of community spirit and sharing is so important when you are relatively recently arrived in a country and it is hard to get established. The Charles family were from Trinidad and were another of the families that always used to come to my parents' Saturday-night parties.

In Kingston, we stayed with the family of my sister's best university friend, Beverley Randall. Mum had been very kind and welcoming to Beverley when she was studying in England, making her part of the family in her inimitable way, so the Randalls were happy to return the favour. Theirs was a lovely house in a district called Greenwich Farm and Mrs Randall spent all her time sitting peacefully in her rocking chair on the veranda, watching the world go by in the street outside. I expect that was the sort of peaceful life Mum and Dad were imagining they would achieve for themselves once they had built their house.

The two families had known each other since before Mum and Dad even came to England the first time, and Beverley lived with us in the holidays when she came over to study: yet another person cheerfully crammed into our overcrowded living space. Because she was older than me, Mum insisted that I show her 'respect', which meant I had to call her 'Sister Beverley' and not just 'Beverley'. When she graduated from university, she went to Miami to become a nurse, which seemed incredibly exciting to me because America was where all the best music seemed to come from. It was like some distant promised land that I dreamed of one day visiting.

After a few weeks, Dad managed to rent us a room of our own in Acacia Gardens, a nice middle-class suburb of Kingston, which we moved into while he set about building us a house of our own on a plot in Spanish Town, an area where the singer Grace Jones was born and lived until she was 17, when she moved to New York with her parents and grew up to become a complete legend.

As usual, things didn't work out quite as smoothly as Dad had hoped and it wasn't long before the money started to run out and we had to go back to the Randalls while the builders continued to work on the house in the sun at their leisurely local pace.

Some of Dad's original dry-cleaning businesses on the island had closed down without him there to oversee them, but a few still had customers and so he hired new people and tried to get everything up and running again as it had been before he left for England. He was always looking for new business ideas, talking to people, dreaming of making it big, imagining that he was about to solve all his problems and become a wealthy man. At one stage, he even opened a bar in a premises next to one of the dry-cleaning businesses. He stocked it up and there was a big opening night with free food and drink for all comers, which attracted freeloaders from all over Kingston. It wasn't unlike the sort of parties he and Mum used to throw in England on Saturday nights except that I didn't know all the people who came to drink with him at the bar. Dad was in his element as the owner and the centre of attention and everyone went away having had a fantastic night out at his expense. But I think that that was the only marketing idea he had managed to come up with for the venture because nothing much seemed to happen after that and there never seemed to be many customers.

Dad was always coming up with ideas, always busy, always talking to people, but he never laid proper plans or did any research or took good business advice. As I grew older, I noticed that he always seemed to end up floundering at everything he tried, moving on from one thing to another with a great fanfare of optimism. A few months after its riotous launch, I wandered into the bar and went behind the counter to get myself a soft drink, as I often did.

'Your dad doesn't own this place any more,' a woman leaning on the bar told me.

It was the first I'd heard of it. I think there may have been some problems with his licence but, whatever the reason, that was the end of another of his little dreams.

He was a very stubborn man and would never listen to anyone if they weren't telling him what he wanted to hear, so a lot of the time Mum gave up bothering and just let him get on with things. He didn't get violent with her, like a lot of men do with their wives if they don't agree with them, but he would shout so loudly that it was impossible for anyone else to make themselves heard and so he would always win any argument.

That trip was my first time abroad, which made it an even more intense and exotic experience to my young eyes. I can remember so many vivid details from the moment we first landed, coming out of the plane into the unexpected heat and gazing around me at the airport shacks and what looked like jungle foliage beyond. A porter in the little airport building tried to persuade Mum to allow him to take her bag, and I remember her sending him on his way, telling him he was charging too much, that she could 'carry her own bag, thank you very much'.

Despite the heat and the tropical look of the place with its palm trees and colourful local people, the thing that struck me first as we drove through the streets of Kingston was that I couldn't see any fish and chip shops or Wimpy Bars. To be deprived of the places that had always brought me the most comfort in my young life was disquieting and immediately I began to worry.

The mood of the spoiled little girl who had been brought up pretty much as an only child, allowed to have whatever she wanted, grew gradually darker in the following days. I threw tantrums at the slightest provocation, like when they told me there wasn't a sweet shop in Kingston and I was just going to have to eat fresh fruit like everyone else. As the weeks went by and I grew increasingly hot and hungry and bored, I was making life hell for everyone. I was determined to force them into taking me home to England, where I would be able to indulge myself with all the things I was used to. The only advantage to all this deprivation, as I saw it, was that I slimmed right down for the first time I could remember.

Despite my tantrums, Dad was determined to make a life for us on the island. He refused to listen to my pleadings to be returned home and enrolled me in a local school, confident that I would get used to the idea eventually, once I had made some new friends. In England I had been very happy at school, so that wasn't a problem to me, until my first day at my new school. What I hadn't been prepared for was that to the other children I would seem very different, an object ripe for derision. At my school in London, I had been pretty much like everyone else, but in Jamaica I appeared to be a spoiled little rich girl, and they instantly hated me for it. Things that I would never have given a second thought to at my old school, like the fact that Dad had his Hillman Hunter shipped over from England and drove me to and from the school gates in it each day, made me look really pampered compared with everyone else, as they had to walk everywhere and didn't have their parents watching over them every second of the day. The fact that I was wearing normal leather shoes, bought from Clarks back in England, also marked me out as being different from the others, who came to class in worn-down slippers, sandals or even bare feet, and they set about making my life a misery at every opportunity.

'You're a rich bitch, with your leather shoes and being driven to school!' they taunted.

'You must be some kind of millionairess!'

'Give us some of your money!'

Mum would pack me up a nice lunch each day, making me different from the others yet again, but she didn't give me any money, so I had nothing I could give my tormentors to make them leave me alone, and that made them even angrier. To begin with, it was only one or two of them picking on me, but the feeling of hatred towards me seemed to spread and before long virtually every child was throwing abuse in my direction. Even some of the teachers seemed to think I was some sort of lowlife, singling me out in front of the class for humiliation.

'Is that your real hair, girl? Let's have a look and see.'

In class, I was a hard worker, so I had some protection there, but in the playground I was totally exposed and the bullies had free access to me with no restraint from adults. I realised that I needed to find someone to look after me if

I didn't want to end up being teased and maybe even physically hurt every day. Some enterprising local traders had set up stalls all round the grounds to sell snacks and books and stationery to the kids because the school was too poor to supply anything for free. In a poor society, there are always street traders ready to fill every gap and cater for every need, desperate to make a little money to live on, always struggling through one day at a time. This was my chance to find some protection against my tormentors. Plucking up all my courage, I went to a man who was selling stationery.

'Can I help you during playtime?' I asked.

'Sure,' he grinned, probably spotting that I was a lonely little fat girl in need of a friend. 'You can stand there and watch the stall. Make sure the kids don't steal the rubbers and stuff.'

It was a relief not just to have a friend and ally, but also to have something to do during the breaks since I didn't have any friends to play with. From then on, the moment the bell went for break time I would head to the stall and help the trader, making sure that I stayed close and that everyone could see he was my friend. He was pleased with the arrangement too because he found that his profits actually went up with me guarding his merchandise. The others couldn't touch me as long as I was around a grown-up, and I got free stationery in exchange for my services, but of course it didn't help me to integrate myself with the other kids and probably made them hate me all the more.

Dad was always surrounded by loads of hangers-on wherever he went, because they all thought he had money and hoped some of it would rub off on them. Compared with the rest of them, I suppose he had. He did nothing to discourage them because he liked to be the centre of attention and to have everyone listening to his words of wisdom, laughing at his jokes. Most of them, however, were pretty unreliable friends. He was out drinking with one of them one time and the guy, who had probably had far more to drink than he should have done, took the keys to the Hillman without asking, drove off at speed and ended up crashing it into a petrol station. He was lucky to get out alive, but the car was a write-off and I don't think Dad had any insurance. People seemed to be very casual about things like insurance in Jamaica.

We might have seemed rich to the other kids, but we certainly didn't have enough money to buy another car when everything we had was going into building the house. Not having a car any more meant that I had to start travelling on the school bus with my tormentors, which was like hell because it meant they had me totally at their mercy and it was impossible for me to escape their taunts and threats. I might have found a way to make my lunchtimes and breaks safe, but I still lived in fear of being caught on my own by the others. My life was such a misery that eventually I told Mum I wasn't going to go to school any more.

'I want to go back to England,' I told her firmly. 'I want to go back to my old school. I was so happy there.'

She must have been able to see that I was serious, because she told me I didn't have to go to that school any more.

'We'll find you somewhere else,' she promised.

It was such a relief to be able to stay at home and not

face all the bullies. But finding somewhere else for me to go was never going to be easy, especially when Mum and Dad were distracted with the problems of building the house, and a year later I was still at home every day and still miserable. I didn't waste my days completely, because I had plenty of time to read books, but in other ways my education ground to a halt as Mum searched in vain for a suitable school. I didn't care how long it took. It was too hot for school anyway and if I had to be in Jamaica I was perfectly happy to laze around in the shade all day, chatting to the neighbours, who were all a great deal friendlier towards me than the kids at school had been.

That year the workmen finally finished building our new home, a beautiful wooden house. The results were impressive, even if it had taken a lot longer than Dad had originally anticipated. To me it seemed like the poshest house in the area, partly because it was the only new building and partly because it was such a nice grey colour, with smart red doors and white windows. People actually used to gather at the metal gates to the courtyard just to stare at it and take pictures, which made me feel very proud. No one would want to take pictures of it now because it is so rundown and the whole area round it has gone to seed. It's hard to keep things nice in Jamaica when the sun is so hot and the rain storms are so fierce, and no one ever seems to have any money for repairs or enough energy for regular maintenance work.

Outside of school, I did manage to make friends with a few people of my age. There was a boy called David Burke, who was six years older than me and lived in the next big house down the road. He first got my attention by throwing bottle tops at me, which I thought was quite funny but which made Dad so angry that he forbade me to talk to him again. It was probably just an excuse: I think Dad would have forbidden me to talk to any boy at that stage, however well behaved he might have been. I guess all fathers can remember what they were like when they were boys and want to protect their daughters from the truth.

But David was too full of self-confidence to allow himself to be intimidated by Dad, and persisted in coming to our gate most days, sometimes on his own and sometimes with a group of other boys. When Dad arrived home unexpectedly one day and found me out there with them all, he completely lost his temper and stormed straight into the house, leaving me frozen to the spot in horror at what might be in store. Having grabbed a leather belt he came running back out and set about beating me with it, shouting and flailing about and putting on a show in front of the whole street. It was the only time he ever hit me and I was mortified, not so much because it hurt but because everyone else was laughing and pointing as he whacked me, knowing that I was too fat to be able to run away.

It was perfectly normal to see Jamaican fathers doling out corporal punishment to their children, but it was unusual for Dad, and in any case I thought it was really unfair. I hadn't even been doing anything bad with David and his friends, but the rule was that I was never allowed to play with boys, no exceptions. I think it was the fact that I had directly disobeyed him that really made Dad angry because normally I was a pretty obedient child, for all my tantrums. Humiliated at being made such a spectacle of, I burst into tears and ran indoors to escape the jeering of the crowd with Dad in full pursuit, shouting and lashing out at me. It was the only time I can remember him raising his hand to me, or to anyone else for that matter.

Dad installed a dry-cleaning and pressing machine in an annex on the side of the house to provide a service to the local neighbourhood. Once people heard that he was there, they all started using his services and from then on he was always to be found in the annex, working. He was passionate about the way he turned out the clothes and justly proud of the way he presented them back to their owners. I still think of him whenever I pass a dry cleaner's and catch the familiar scent of the chemicals and solvents they use. He always smelled like that when he came back from work, as if he had been personally cleaned and pressed.

Being surrounded by older relatives and listening to them talk and reminisce about the past, I began to learn more about my family history. Dad's mother had come to Jamaica from India when she was young. I guess they must have been a trading family, or maybe they came as indentured servants after slavery was abolished. Dad always told us that his mother was stunningly beautiful and that all the local men wanted to marry her.

'There were a lot of people who were jealous of your grandfather when she chose him from among all her suitors,' he would tell me. 'Some jealous person decided that if they couldn't have her no one would. So they put poison in her food and she died. After that my father left Jamaica and went to live in Cuba.'

To a young girl's ears, it seemed a sad but romantic story. My grandmother was only 33 years old when she died, but she had already had three children. My father, his brother and his sister were then brought up by their maternal grandparents on the Indian side of the family when their father left for Cuba. It wasn't unusual in the Caribbean for the grandparents to play a major role in bringing up children while the parents went off to be the breadwinners for the whole family. Maybe it was memories of what his grandparents had done for him that was part of the reason why Dad was so supportive of me when I was later left on my own with my four kids.

I remember meeting his Indian grandmother, who didn't die until she was 105 and seemed to me to be the oldest person in the world. A lot of the members of Dad's family lived to fabulously great ages. There seems to be no rhyme or reason as to why some people are chosen to live two or even three times as long as others.

CHAPTER SIX

THE ZAVARONI FACTOR

Mum must have finally decided that I was never going to acclimatise to Jamaica and that she wasn't going to be able to find me a school where I would fit in, or maybe she wanted to get back to London herself to see my grandmother and needed an excuse. Whatever the reason, she told me that we were going back.

By this time, Dad's dry-cleaning business in the annex was going well, because he was working so hard at it, and so it was decided that he would stay on longer to make a bit more money to help us re-establish ourselves in England, while Mum would take me back home on the *Begona*, the same ship that had brought them to Southampton all those years before. Although I would have preferred it if we had all travelled together, I was overjoyed at the thought of getting back to the land of Wimpy Bars and Radio 1. I was also excited at the thought of travelling back on a ship that looked to me like a luxurious floating skyscraper.

In reality, of course, the *Begona* was by no means a cruise liner, but it still seemed as sumptuous as the *Titanic* to my impressionable young eyes as I walked around the decks and the beautifully decorated rooms, as awestruck as Leonardo DiCaprio's character is in the film when he stumbles across the upper-class accommodation. Compared with the rush and worry of air travel, with crowded airports and packed planes, going by boat is a very leisurely way to travel and a bit like stepping back into another age.

On the way home, we stopped off at exotic-sounding places like Trinidad, Venezuela, Curacao and Portugal to take on more passengers and to let others off. The trip gave me the opportunity to tell people I had been to all these countries, although in some of them we didn't even get off the ship but just gazed out from the rails over the busy docks and distant tropical vistas as people bustled up and down the gangplanks and luggage was loaded and unloaded, everyone excited about arriving in new places, starting new lives or being reunited with loved ones. The world and its wide-open oceans suddenly seemed very big and exciting to a little girl who had seen nothing much beyond her local streets in north London and Kingston, Jamaica.

When we eventually docked at Southampton and were all standing at the rails watching what was going on as usual, waiting to be told when we could disembark, there was a lot of shouting and the police rushed aboard to arrest some people, accusing them of trying to smuggle drugs into the country. It felt like being part of one of the popular shows that I was sometimes allowed to watch if we were visiting someone with a television set, series with titles like *Z-Cars* or *Softly, Softly.*

It felt so good to see the familiar sights of England again, without a palm tree or fresh-fruit seller in sight. My only regret at leaving Jamaica was that we had been given a couple of mongrel dogs, called Fluffy and Whitey, who I loved beyond all reason. It had been painful parting from them, especially when they ran happily along behind the taxi as we drove off, barking joyfully and obviously not realising that I was deserting them for ever. It weighed heavily on my heart that I had proved to be a bad friend to them after they had shown me so much unconditional love and it still makes me sad to think about them, even all these years later.

The moment we arrived back in London, I immediately felt like I was home and safe and I experienced an almost physical lifting of my spirits, despite the fact that the country was in a right mess at the time, with the miners on strike and millions of people working a three-day week. The authorities used to turn the power off in the evenings in different areas and when it was our turn we would have to make do with candles. It was quite exciting for a child, but yet another annoyance to grown-ups like my mother: for her it was already hard to find enough hours in the day for everything she needed to get done. One of the reasons for immigrating to a country like England was to have reliable services like electricity. Even the dustbin men were going on strike and there were piles of black plastic sacks all over the streets, waiting to be collected, making London feel more like something from the Third World than one of the great centres of European civilisation.

To make things even worse, the IRA was at the height of its bombing campaign against London and other English cities like Guildford and Birmingham. Meanwhile, the infamous 'revolutionary socialist' Rose Dugdale was actually operating from Tottenham, an area we were all too familiar with, and ended up being imprisoned in Ireland at the end of the year.

But none of this could bring me down because I was back in the land of Wimpy Bars and pick'n'mix sweets and was soon cheerfully piling the weight back on. This was a time when Elton John was pounding out 'Bennie and the Jets' and 'Goodbye Yellow Brick Road', David Essex was taking my breath away with 'Rock On' and Terry Jacks was singing about 'Seasons in the Sun'. Olivia Newton-John was at the height of her fame and Barbra Streisand was outselling everyone with 'The Way We Were'. Stevie Wonder was pretty much summing up how I felt about being back in London with his hit 'Living for the City'.

Mum and I wanted to return to the same area in north London that we had known before and I definitely wanted to go back to my old school, but there was no chance we were going to be able to buy anything now that Dad had sunk all his money into building the new house in Kingston. So initially we had to find a roof wherever we could and another friend of my sister's agreed to rent us a room in her house in Plumstead in south-east London.

Since I didn't know any other children in the area, I spent a fair bit of time in the house on my own to begin with. Exploring upstairs one day I opened the door to a spare bedroom, which was completely filled with piles of old newspapers. Mum had told me that I wasn't allowed in there, probably worried that it would seem to our hosts like I was prying into their private lives, but I couldn't resist the temptation. Once I had found this wealth of information just waiting for me to explore further I crept back in there whenever I was able to get away from the grown-ups. I would sit for hours picking up one paper after another, reading the front-page news about the strikes and the bombs and the trouble in Northern Ireland, catching up on everything that I had missed while we had been away in the Caribbean.

I was starting to get an idea of how the grown-up world around me worked and I was thirsty to learn and understand more. Some of the things I read were frightening too. There was one particularly nasty story at the time about the murder of a child called Maria Caldwell and I remember being unable to stop myself from reading about it even though it terrified me to think that such things could happen to little girls like me. I had led such a sheltered, protected life I had no idea such wicked things actually happened. I can still picture her little face staring out from those grey pages of newsprint, a very personal little tale of tragedy nestling among all the big political stories of the day.

Although we had to live most of the time in the one room that we were renting, I could use the host family's sitting room to watch television with the three other girls in the house in the evenings, and it was there that I discovered what I wanted to do with the rest of my life. It was a bit of an epiphany for me, a moment of shocking clarity and intense excitement which has lived in my memory ever since.

There was a very popular programme at the time called *Opportunity Knocks*, which was a talent competition similar to the big shows that Simon Cowell makes today, hosted by a man called Hughie Green. Hughie was later revealed as the father of the late Paula Yates, Bob Geldof's first wife. Until a newspaper revealed everything, Paula had believed her father was her mother's husband, another television presenter, Jess Yates. Paula had first became really famous herself in the 1980s when she presented the music show *The Tube* with Jools Holland, and went on to front *The Big Breakfast* in the 1990s. She died tragically from a heroin overdose when she was just 41 after enduring innumerable newspaper scandals about her family and about her own private life. Paula's mother had been a showgirl and theirs was a family that lived in the limelight and, like so many others, was eventually destroyed by it. I knew none of this, of course, at the time I was watching *Opportunity Knocks*. As far as I and most of the viewing population were concerned, Hughie Green was an avuncular, if rather oily, television presenter who hosted this programme and a popular quiz show called *Double Your Money*.

He had started out as a child star himself and had his own BBC radio show at just 14. He had also had his own all-children touring concert party called *Hughie Green and His Gang* and appeared in a few films, including *Tom Brown's Schooldays*. After a few years in Canada, where he took Canadian nationality and picked up his trademark

Above left: Ivy Ewen, my mum. Mum and Dad arrived in England in 1958, dreaming of a better future.

Above right: Two years old, playing with dolly on the wall outside our house in Finsbury Park. That's my Grandma in the background with the broom.

Below: A cuddle for my cat, Mary Jane. Mary Jane was actually a male cat, but I was adamant that he should have a girl's name!

Above left: Mum holds baby Euphemia (it was only later that I started to use the name Melissa).

Above right: With my two sisters, Sonia (left) and Francis (right)

Below left: I loved school and was even chosen to appear in the film of the Queen's visit

Below right: My grandmother, Isilda Cecilia Russell. She was the first ever West Indian classical pianoforte teacher in England. Both Alex and I seem to have inherited her musical talent!

Above left: In Jamaica with my nephew Camilo.

Above right: Don't make me go! On the way to the airport in 1977 – I desperately didn't want to go back to Jamaica.

Below left: Growing up – me aged 15. I'm the one on the far right, with the 'Purdy' hairstyle.

Below right: My sister Frances in 1979. She has now sadly passed away.

Me and my music.

Above: Angie Brown congratulates me after my first ever appearance at Voices open mic night – I got a standing ovation!

Inset: The first band I was in, Impulse. I was 18 when I joined them, after I had sung at a party.

Below left: With saxophonist Mike Parlett at a charity event.

Below right: Dancing with Paul Young in Abu Dhabi.

A publicity shot from my singing days.

My babies!

Above left: Sheniece, my eldest, at 12 weeks old.

Above right: The kids tucking into breakfast with their dad.

Below: Clockwise from left: Sheniece, David, Alex and Aaron.

ome pictures from my family album.

Above left: My dad, Ivan Ewen.

Above right: Me posing on some fishing nets!

Below left: My older son David on the beach with his grandma in Tenerife.

Below right: My wonderful parents.

Above: This picture is terrible as it was taken on my phone. But it's from the amazing night I sang with Stevie Wonder. I'm in the middle and Lennox Lewis is on the right. What an experience!

Below: In Jordan for a friend's wedding. In the photo on the right, I was on my way to see Petra.

Above left: Sheniece and David 'look after' Alex.

Above right: David tries out his sea legs on a day trip to France.

Middle: Doing a bit of shopping in Tunisia.

Left: In Lanzarote with a tiny Aaron.

Above left: A sad day at my Mum's funeral. Sheniece, David and Alex are standing with my nephew Milo.

Above right: Alex with David and Aaron on a family holiday to America.

Below: When she was just 12 years old, Alex got through to the final of the BBC's *Star for a Night*, along with Joss Stone. On the left of the picture is my Dad and the tall guy next to him is my nephew, Camilo. Alex is in the middle with her thumbs up, Aaron is in front of her next to his friend Tim, and big sister Sheniece has her arm around Alex. My son, David is on the far right, next to Sheniece.

…amily holidays to Jamaica. *Above*: Cooling off with Alex and Sheniece and, *below*, with slightly older Alex.

Above: Doing what I love best.

Below: Family and friends turned out to support Alex in the *X Factor* – we are all so proud of her.

accent, he returned to London in the late 1940s and soon began to make a name for himself in the new but fast-growing world of television.

Opportunity Knocks already had a long history of finding talent and launching people's careers. Stars who had started out on the programme included a huge singing star of the 1950s called Frankie Vaughan, who came second on the show as part of a duet and went on to become known as 'Mr Moonlight', high stepping through his routines with a cane and boater; comedian Les Dawson and a Welsh folk singer called Mary Hopkin. Mary was spotted singing on the show by Paul McCartney, who immediately signed her to the Beatles' new Apple label and gave her a nostalgic song called 'Those Were the Days', which became a massive hit on both sides of the Atlantic in 1968. The programme was just as much of a star-making factory as *The X Factor* or *American Idol* are today.

Sandie Shaw also released a version of the song, but, despite the fact she was already an established star, having won *The Eurovision Song Contest* with the incredibly popular 'Puppet on a String' the previous year, it was Mary Hopkin's version which the public really took to. Just like today, there were some people in the music industry who didn't believe that winners of talent contests should be allowed to compete with 'professional' stars when it came to chart success. Then, as now, the great British record-buying public disagreed. They knew what they liked and they went out to buy it in their millions.

Opportunity Knocks had started out as a radio show on the BBC in the 1940s and then moved to Radio

Luxembourg, which was one of the first commercial radio stations, broadcasting out of Europe when it was still illegal for any radio stations apart from the BBC to broadcast in Britain. Contestants would appear in front of a live audience and at the end of the show Hughie Green would ask the audience to applaud each act and they would measure the level of the applause on his 'clapometer' to try to predict the winner. But the actual winner was chosen by the public, who sent their votes in through the post, 'in their own handwriting' in order to prevent vote-rigging scandals. It seems almost unbelievably primitive compared with today's phone-voting systems (phone voting was only introduced in the late 1980s, when *Opportunity Knocks* was revived and presented by Bob Monkhouse).

Along with most other young people, I absolutely loved the show, religiously tuning in with the other girls in the house every week, speculating and arguing about which of the acts we believed would be coming back after the previous week's voting.

On one of his shows in 1974, Hughie introduced the public to a little Scottish girl who was more or less the same age as me. She was called Lena Zavaroni. Although she was only nine years old, this little girl had the most incredibly mature singing voice. She came on screen, brimming with confidence, belted out 'Mama, He's Making Eyes at Me', and stunned both the live audience and the television viewers with a voice every bit as strong as most of the pop stars of the day.

As I watched her, so transfixed I was hardly even remembering to breathe, I felt like I had suddenly seen my whole future flashing before me. I longed with every fibre of my body to be up there in Lena's place. I wanted to be strutting across a stage in front of the cameras and the live audience with all eyes on me. Although I had been obsessed with music for several years by then, it hadn't occurred to me that someone like me could actually turn it into a career. All the singers had seemed so grown up, glamorous and sophisticated, a million miles from anything I could identify with in my own life. How could I even think about comparing myself to stars like Barbra Streisand or Diana Ross? But watching Lena, who looked like every 'girl next door', suddenly opened all the doors in my mind and I was flooded with feelings of excitement and anticipation at what glories might lie ahead of me. If she could do it, why shouldn't I be able to?

'I could go on that show,' I blurted out to the others as Lena's joyful and uplifting performance came to an end, my heart pounding in my chest as I listened to the applause, imagining how it would feel if it was for me. 'What do you think I should do? Should I sing or should I dance?'

'You can't do either,' the others laughed. 'You're just fat.'

They weren't being cruel in the way the kids at the school in Kingston had been: they were just being matter-of-fact. I took no notice. I was too high on my own excitement for them to be able to bring me down that easily. In my heart I was sure that this was the sort of thing I was going to be doing with my life. I was going to be a performer and I just *had* to find a way to make it possible. I guess that similar dreams lurk in the hearts of millions of little girls, although none of them has the slightest idea of what obstacles lie ahead on such a path and of how difficult it will be for them to break through in order to get noticed and prove themselves to the world. When you are a child, you are sure things are somehow going to be different for you.

So many innocent childhood dreams can lead to disappointment, but every so often someone like Lena comes along and makes anything seem possible for a while. At least that's how it seemed to me as I sat watching the flickering old black-and-white television, willing the clapometer to go higher and higher as the smirking master of ceremonies urged the audience to show their appreciation.

I dare say I could have got on to *Opportunity Knocks*, or its rival, *New Faces*, if I had auditioned for them. But when it came down to it I never actually had the guts to apply, which is where most people fall by the wayside when it comes to taking the first step of turning their dreams into reality. *New Faces* was launched in 1973 on ITV, with the catchy theme tune 'You're a Star', sung by Carl Wayne, who had previously been part of the Move. Where Hughie Green was always effusively encouraging to all the acts on his show, *New Faces* had a panel of judges (a bit like the BBC's *Juke Box Jury* before it), who could sometimes be very cutting in their comments. Tony Hatch, a famous songwriter of the time, did much the same job of puncturing the unrealistic dreams of the less talented performers as Simon Cowell does today. In 1975, Marti Caine, a singer and comedienne, beat Lenny Henry and Victoria Wood to win the show and later came back as the presenter. Other winners included Michael Barrymore (who went on to front popular amateur talent shows of his own on television, *My Kind of People* and *My Kind of Music*, which Susan Boyle actually entered in 1995, singing 'I Don't Know How to Love Him', many years before her triumph on *Britain's Got Talent*). Another was Patti Boulaye, who was the only act on *New Faces* ever to receive the maximum number of points that the judges were allowed to give.

Although it was fun living in Plumstead, the journey to school each day on the other side of London was a nightmare, and after a while Mum and I moved in with my grandmother, sharing the room she was still renting from the Charles family in Tottenham. Now there were three of us in the bed instead of two because the room was too small for any more furniture to be fitted in, but it didn't worry me because I was used to it and it made me feel secure to wake up each morning tucked up between Mum and Grandma. Money was tight all the time but Mum got a job as an auxiliary nurse at University College Hospital in Gower Street and we just got on with life as best we could, never really questioning the way things were, cheerfully accepting whatever life had to throw at us.

My obsession with music and singing was growing all the time and I started buying a magazine called *Disco 45*, which was published throughout the 1970s, until *Smash Hits* came along and put it out of business. As well as photos and personal ads, *Disco 45* also printed all the lyrics of the popular songs of the time and I would read and learn them so that I could sing along with the stars when they came on the radio, concentrating on making my voice sound as much like them as possible. I was first surprised, then pleased, to find that I was good at it.

Grandma fell out with the Charles family soon after we got there, although I never quite understood why, and we all had to move out. She went to a flat in Haringey and Mum and I rented a room from another West Indian family, the Johns, who lived in the Caledonian Road in Islington. Their house was quite close to where I live now, not far from the notorious Pentonville Prison, which was where the mass murderers Crippen and Christie were both hanged and where more recently Pete Doherty, Boy George and Amy Winehouse's husband, Blake Fielder-Civil, all served sentences. Despite having such ominous neighbours, it's a nice area and it would be home to my family for many years to come as we dreamed our dreams and struggled to stay afloat.

CHAPTER SEVEN

WANNABE ROCK STAR

It wasn't long before Dad followed us back from Jamaica and there was no longer enough room for all of us in the one bed. Squeezing in with Mum and Grandma had been one thing, squeezing in between Mum and Dad was quite another. I'm guessing that, after being apart from Mum for so long, Dad was also keen to get them some space to themselves. Whatever the reason, he went out and bought me a folding bed, which could be packed away during the day for me to use as a table. I was beside myself with happiness at this development, which seemed to me to mark a major milestone in my grindingly slow journey towards adulthood. I loved that folding bed more than any possession I had ever had before, and I kept it for more than 30 years. I've lost count of the number of people who have slept on it over those years. It was the first time I had ever had my own bed.

Dad seemed to be happy to be back in England and the Cypriot family who ran the Alex Dry Cleaners chain were happy to give him his old job back as soon as he informed them he had returned. I imagine it isn't that easy to find pressers as good and as popular with the customers as Dad was. It must have been a relief for Mum to have another income coming in as she can't have been earning very much from her nursing. Having struggled as a single mother myself for many years now, I can appreciate what it must have been like for her having all the responsibility for looking after me while Dad was still in the Caribbean.

As so often happened, I reckon things can't have gone as well for him in Kingston as he had hoped. Building the house had taken longer than he had expected and must have used up all the money he had saved from selling the house in London, putting him right back to square one financially. Although he had plenty of customers for the dry cleaning, they probably weren't able to afford to pay the sort of rates you need to make a business like that profitable in the long term, when you have to buy or rent the machines and the chemicals. But Dad was never a man to dwell on his disappointments, always thinking about the next thing he was going to do, looking forward to the future and full of optimism all the time. I expect he thought he would rebuild his fortunes in London, just as he had done before. But perhaps he was forgetting that this time he wasn't bringing any money in from Jamaica with him, and that he now had a child to support and a wife who was not as fit and strong as she had been the first time she had stepped off the *Begona* at Southampton nearly 20 years before.

From my point of view, one of the best parts of having him back was the tickets that he was given once more by grateful stars coming in from the Rainbow next door. They always seemed to take to Dad. People as varied as the Jackson Five, Gary Glitter and Lulu all remembered him and asked for him by name when they brought their clothes in. Lulu was particularly kind to him and gave him tickets several times. I became her greatest fan from listening to her in those concerts. In fact, I still am. I think she has the most fantastic voice and has lost none of her vocal power with age. Years later, when I was working at Marks & Spencer, I actually got to serve her. I was so awestruck to find myself face to face with my idol that I didn't manage to raise enough courage to tell her how much her music had meant to me over the years, or what an impact she'd had on me as a child. Later still, my eldest daughter, Sheniece, got a job in one of those really posh lingerie shops and Lulu was her personal customer. Sheniece actually had to take all the personal measurements of my greatest heroine. Even though she's now turned 60, Lulu still looks fantastic.

It was when we got back to London from Jamaica that I'd fallen totally in love with the Bay City Rollers, a teeny-bopper pop group from Scotland who were all the rage with young girls at the time. I was particularly mad about the drummer, Derek Longmuir, who was the brother of the bassist. I mean, I loved them all, but I think I was actually 'in love' with Derek, with all the yearning passion of an overweight teenage girl who likes to dream impossible dreams without having the slightest idea how to make them a reality, or indeed any real wish to do so. I don't think anyone ever forgets their first love, even if the love object is some totally unobtainable pop or film star and the whole romance happens inside their head.

I was by no means the only one suffering in this way. The media was full of stories about 'Rollermania', likening it to the 'Beatlemania' the same journalists had invented and written about in the 1960s, with all the usual pictures of crowds of screaming, fainting girls at concerts and airports and anywhere else they could catch up with their idols. The group had a number of huge-selling records and made a television series called *Shang-a-Lang*, named after one of their biggest hits. Clive Davis of Arista Records (who would discover Whitney Houston a few years later) launched them in America, where they also went to the top of the charts.

Dad knew all about my crush – everyone around me did – and he made me an outfit like the ones the group wore on stage. It was basically a white shirt and white trousers, trimmed with tartan along the seams and the cuffs, using tartan scarves from Chapel Market that he would cut into strips.

Chapel Market in Islington is one of the great traditional London markets, full of fruit and veg stalls, fishmongers and wide boys selling anything and everything you could ever want. There is also a good old-fashioned pie and mash vendor which has been there for over a hundred years and is still one of my favourite eating places in the world.

Dad even cut the group's name out in tartan and sewed it on across my chest, in case anyone was in any doubt about who I was trying to emulate. Whenever I went out of the house in my new gear, Mum would put my hair into four fat plaits, tying them up with ribbons. I must have looked a complete sight, but I felt great.

I absolutely loved that outfit and wore it every day for ages, without the slightest idea how stupid I must have appeared to everyone who wasn't a 'Rollermaniac'. I would happily walk the streets in it, which, considering I had become overweight again pretty quickly after our return to England, must have been a startling sight. Most people were polite enough not to laugh as I trotted proudly past, but I do remember getting some bad comments thrown at me by a group of young black guys who thought I was a 'stupid bitch' for liking 'white music'. I was shocked by their comments, mainly because it hadn't yet occurred to me that there was any difference between 'black' and 'white' music, but also because I still never really thought of myself as being black. Although their comments disappointed me and made me think about a few things, they still didn't put me off wearing the outfit. Nothing could have put me off that. In fact, I probably liked the idea of having to suffer some abuse for the loves of my life, playing the little martyr.

When I stopped to think about it, I realised that there was a lot of 'white' music that I liked, such as the songs of David Essex and Neil Sedaka, that many black kids despised for not being 'cool' enough. I didn't care because I knew what I liked and I was used to not being 'cool'. David Essex made a film around that time, the mid-1970s, called *Stardust*, in which he played a rock star. The posters carried the tag line 'Show me a boy who never wanted to be a rock star and I'll show you a liar'. One of his biggest hits was called 'Gonna Make You a Star', which he wrote himself and was a satirical look at his own success and all the sniping criticism that he got from rock-music snobs. He may have been sending himself and the business up a bit, but I took the whole thing very seriously indeed. I could completely understand the concept of someone wanting to be a rock star.

Dad was still being incredibly protective of me after he came back to England, even though he'd had no way of knowing what I was up to throughout the months that we had been apart. He still didn't like me to visit other people's houses on my own. I don't know what he was frightened of any more because there weren't any boys hanging around me like there had been in Kingston, just a bunch of other schoolgirls who all wanted to go around together and gossip and listen to music. I never wanted to upset Dad, because of all the shouting (and the memory of his leather belt in Kingston), and because I was basically an obedient child, but when a friend called Christine asked me back to her family's flat to watch her new colour television I couldn't resist the temptation, especially as I knew that Dad was still at work and wouldn't have to find out.

Watching programmes in colour was a novelty to me and I was happy to sit staring at virtually anything that came on, but Christine soon grew restless with our inactivity and got out a tape recorder for us to play with.

'Shall we do some singing?' she suggested hopefully.

'OK,' I said, intrigued enough to tear my eyes away from the screen as she pushed a cassette into the recorder.

Because I had memorised so many hit songs from the

pages of my *Disco 45* magazines, it was easy to find one that I could sing all the way through into the tape machine without any backing track. I decided to do 'Rock Me Gently', which was a huge hit for a Canadian singer-songwriter called Andy Kim. It was also covered by Neil Diamond, which turned it into a classic that still gets played a lot on the radio today. Not understanding any of the sexual innuendo hidden in the lyrics, I innocently sang my heart out, pleased to see that Christine was surprised and impressed by what she was hearing. When we played the recording back, I was surprised myself by how good it sounded and I left Christine's house with a feeling of excitement bubbling away inside me at the thought that I was actually good at something which I loved doing. Maybe, I told myself, it wasn't such a wild idea after all to think that I could perform on television.

What I didn't know, until the headmaster called me into his office a week or so later, was that Christine had taken the tape into school and played it to him, or to someone on the staff who had then passed it on to him. When I initially received the summons to go and see him, I thought I must have done something wrong, but I couldn't imagine what it could be since I had never knowingly broken any rules.

'I've heard this recording of you singing, Melissa,' he said as I stood trembling in front of him, dreading the thought of what Mum and Dad would say when they heard I had been called in to see the headmaster. 'You've got a good voice. I think you could have a good future.'

It was like a huge weight lifting off my shoulders. It felt so wonderful to have someone grown up say something like that. I had never really thought of myself as having an actual 'future'. I might have fantasised as I sat in front of *Opportunity Knocks* that it was me rather than Lena Zavaroni there on the screen, but to have someone else who I respected say that I was good was something else again. By singing into that little cassette machine, I had inadvertently started to gain a reputation for being a good singer and that was a great feeling.

From then on, the teachers got me to lead the hymn singing at assembly, telling the other children to follow me. By that stage, I'd heard a lot of hymns sung, from going to church with Mum and other family members, and I was well within my vocal comfort zone there. But it was the first time that anyone in any sort of position of authority had actually praised my singing and it made me feel like I could fly. I knew that I could hold a tune because of all the hours I'd spent singing along to the radio. I even thought there might be a possibility that I was good because I was sounding just like the stars I was imitating – people like Aretha Franklin – and I knew for sure they were good, but I hadn't dared to believe that anyone else would ever think I could do it successfully in public.

Aretha is sometimes, and deservedly, called 'The Queen of Soul' and in 2008 *Rolling Stone* magazine named her number one in its list of the 'greatest singers of all time'. Probably her greatest hit was 'Respect', the Otis Redding song that she released in 1967, just in time for the feminist movement to adopt it as a sort of unofficial anthem (even though Otis had originally written it from a man's perspective). It also asks for respect for 'TCP', meaning

'The Coloured People'. *Rolling Stone* had it at number five in its 500 'greatest songs of all time' and it seemed only right that Aretha should be there to sing at President Barack Obama's inauguration in 2009. (In 1993, she had sung at Bill Clinton's first inauguration as well, along with Michael Jackson.)

Aretha sang dozens of great songs, like 'Chain of Fools', 'Say a Little Prayer' and 'You Make Me Feel Like a Natural Woman', and her album *Amazing Grace* sold over two million copies in the US alone, making it the biggest-selling gospel album of all time. She was the daughter of a Baptist minister from Tennessee and was something of a child prodigy for her singing and her piano-playing skills, but she got into trouble as a teenager when she fell pregnant at the age of 13, and then again at 15. Her mother had died in mysterious circumstances when Aretha was just ten, and you can tell from listening to her sing that she is someone who has experienced all the emotions she is singing about. I knew that, if I could do even a passable imitation of a woman that great, I would be doing OK.

Having got a taste for hearing my own voice, and having had my confidence boosted, I nagged Mum into buying me a cassette recorder like Christine's, so that I could record as many songs as I wanted. It felt like having my own little portable studio. I would play the records and then record myself singing along. I would then play back the tapes over and over again, listening intently to myself, trying to improve with each recording, allowing myself to dream of the glittering future that might lie in store for me.

As the years passed, I followed the careers of the many

stars who caught my imagination and I became aware that there was also a dark and dangerous side to stardom, the flip side to all the good stuff on the surface. The launch that *Opportunity Knocks* had given to Lena Zavaroni, for instance, had propelled her to instant stardom but it wasn't long before it became obvious that she was going to be forced to pay a terrible price for that flying start. Her rise was certainly meteoric. Almost everyone in the country knew who she was after she won the show. She became the youngest person ever to get an album in the UK charts and the youngest to appear on the BBC's *Top Of The Pops*, a programme which had already been on air for half an hour every Thursday night for more than ten years by then and had become the Holy Grail of pop music. Lena even got to go to Hollywood and sing with Frank Sinatra and Lucille Ball, appeared on *The Tonight Show* with Johnny Carson, the biggest chat show in America at the time, and performed at the White House for President Ford, and then at the Royal Variety Performance back in London.

Still far too young to leave school, Lena was enrolled at the famous Italia Conti stage school in London, which has been a springboard to fame for so many stars over the decades, from Noel Coward and Gertrude Lawrence before the Second World War to Tracey Ullman and Kelly Brook, Martine McCutcheon and Wendy Richard to Sharon Osbourne and supermodel Naomi Campbell. Naomi is another child of a single Jamaican mother, with a bit of Chinese blood in the mix, who made one of her earliest public appearances at the age of seven in a video for Bob Marley's 'Is This Love?' As well as being the first black supermodel, she also released an album, *Baby Woman*, which sold over a million copies around the world, although it didn't do that well in Britain, and she sang on Vanilla's 'Cool as Ice' track.

If there had ever been a dream career for a star-struck little girl, Lena was living it, and no one watching and listening to her performances could ever have dreamed of how tragically and quickly her life would end.

I never told Mum and Dad about my longing to be like Lena, but I did tell my grandmother during one of my visits to her. I used to get the bus up to see her at weekends and we would sing together in her little retirement flat, where she still had a piano even though she didn't have a television.

'One day we'll be able to do this on stage together,' I would tell her and she would smile indulgently at my big ambitions and pat my hand kindly. Perhaps she had once had dreams like that herself, wishing she was Josephine Baker maybe, or Billie Holiday. When you are young, you never think to ask old people what their dreams were. In fact, when you are young, it is hard to imagine that the old were ever any different from the way you see them, their lives apparently all behind them.

Grandma sang mostly gospel-style hymns, although she wasn't particularly religious herself, even when she was old. Mum and Dad, on the other hand, became more and more religious as they grew older. Dad became a deacon in a local Pentecostal church which had a charismatic preacher who had managed to impress him, and Mum became an avid evangelist for the same church, both of them really getting into the whole Christian thing. Mum even gave up the 'ungodly' habit of smoking cigarettes, although Dad didn't quite manage to go that far. At that stage, I just liked the singing. I've noticed that a lot of West Indian people find God as they grow older, maybe because the seeds were sown by their parents and grandparents when they were young. Many of us reach a stage where life seems to be letting us down a lot and we need something else to believe in in order to have a reason to keep going. If you find you can't call on your fellow man for help and support, you have to look for something or someone else, which leads many of us back to thinking about the being who created us.

Because of our family connections, I got to sing in church a bit, which was fun, but I wasn't allowed to do it as much as I would have liked. After hearing that I liked to sing pop music, the preacher took me to one side and told me that if I was going to raise my voice to the Lord full-time I wasn't allowed to sing anything else.

'If you are going to sing the songs of God,' he warned, 'then you can't sing the songs of the world, like the ones you hear on the radio.'

Since pop music was my greatest love, that wasn't a sacrifice I was willing to make, not even for Him. I wasn't even sure that the preacher was right, although I would never have been disrespectful enough to say anything to his face. It seemed to me that God had made all the songs in the world, even the ones that they played on the radio, and so I couldn't understand how it could be sinful for a little girl with a good voice to want to sing them. In fact, I had a feeling God would like me to sing as many of His songs as I could, but I didn't say anything.

Since Grandma didn't have a television, I had to find other ways to entertain myself while I was there. So, whenever we weren't singing or playing the piano, I would sit down at her table and return to my exercise book, drawing the same faces, making up stories about them, giving them names and taking them on adventures, exercising my imagination, trying out different life stories for them.

Although I loved living as part of such a close-knit family, I was growing increasingly self-conscious about our lack of money when I was among my school friends. I never invited any of them to our home, not wanting them to see how poor we were, all of us living together in one room and still watching a black-and-white television when most of the world had moved on to colour. None of my school friends was rich by any means, but I had been to enough of their homes to know that not many of them had to live like us. It was ironic that I had been driven out of Jamaica because they thought I was a 'rich bitch', whereas in London I was embarrassed by my family's poverty. If my friends said they wanted to come to my home, I would always try to talk them into doing something else, like going ice skating.

That was one of the few social activities that Dad was prepared to allow me out of the house to do with friends on a Saturday morning. I suppose he thought I would be safe in such a public place with so many grown-ups around and with so many layers of protective clothing. It was fantastically exhilarating and I made friends on those mornings that I still see around on the streets today.

In the end, I got really good at it, doing speed skating and even graduated to using ice-hockey skates, which are the ones that don't have any guards on them. The rink used to hire disc jockeys, who played all my favourite disco music at full blast over the speakers while I glided around the ice as if I was as light as a feather. It was like having a soundtrack laid down to my own life. Like I was living in a movie.

CHAPTER EIGHT

MAD ABOUT THE BOY

When Mum told me in 1977 that she and I were going back to Jamaica for a holiday, to check that everything was all right with the house Dad had built and to visit relatives, I was horrified.

Dad had already been back there for a visit on his own, which was fine by me as long as he didn't ask me to go with him, but I think maybe it had been his trip that had made Mum want to do the same. Perhaps she was feeling a bit homesick or nostalgic, or maybe she just fancied a bit of sun and sea and the old reggae lifestyle.

At that stage, I wouldn't have cared if they had told me I was never going to see the place again. Any charms that the laidback lifestyle, warm seas and even the music might have held for me were completely overshadowed by my memories of those terrible school days and the almost constant longings for the fast food that I was pretty much addicted to. Mum, however, had made up her mind and I practically had to be dragged on to the plane kicking and screaming that I didn't want to be parted from my friends and my favourite radio shows. It was the year Julie Covington sang 'Don't Cry for Me, Argentina' and Donna Summer (yet another artist who started out singing in church) had a hit, and such an influence on other musicians, with 'I Feel Love'. Manhattan Transfer were crooning 'Chanson d'Amour' and Abba were topping the charts with one song after another.

Soon after we got to the house in Kingston, I took advantage of being away from Dad's iron rule and announced that I was going to the local shop, hoping I would be able to find something comforting to eat, and left the house before Mum had a chance to protest. On my way down the street, I bumped into David Burke, who I hadn't seen since the previous trip five years before, which may well have been exactly what I was hoping would happen.

By now I was 13, but apparently I looked about 18. David was 19 and looking very good indeed. I have to admit I was instantly knocked out by how handsome he had become since I last saw him. Because he and his family had money, he was by far the best-dressed person in the street and he had all the swagger and confidence you would expect in a handsome boy that age. The first glimpse I got of him as I walked past, he was standing with a friend, astride his bike, looking really sharp.

'Come here, girl,' his big-mouthed friend called over. 'How about me? Choose me.'

'It ain't you that I'll be getting with,' I called back precociously. 'If it's anyone, it'll be him.'

He didn't say anything at the time, but later that night

David sauntered up to the house and leaned nonchalantly against the gate, obviously encouraged by my words earlier, and we started to flirt through the bars. It was like we hadn't been apart at all since our last meeting. We got on well and his visits to the house over the following weeks became a regular habit once more, although he wasn't allowed inside the gates, and if Mum spotted that he had infiltrated the courtyard by even a few inches she would come running out of the house with a broom to shoo him away, no doubt worried what Dad would say if he ever found out she had turned a blind eye to such wicked goings-on. I guess to the experienced eye of a twice-married woman there was no doubt what business a young man like David would have been on, hanging about an impressionable and naïve young girl like me.

Eventually, I managed to convince her that David and I were only talking, and she reluctantly agreed to let him in through the gate, as long as he understood that he could go no further than the courtyard. He may have made it inside the walls of our little citadel, but she still kept a beady eye on him from the window, convinced that sooner or later he was going to bring me trouble, however well he might be pretending to behave now. If she had been able to overhear our conversations, she would have known that he was doing a good job of playing the romantic, flattering me and telling me all the things that an insecure young girl likes to hear. By the end of the six-week holiday, he had convinced me that he thought we should get married as soon as I was old enough.

'I've got things I want to do,' I said when he told me,

flattered and excited by the thought but nervous that I might end up being stampeded into giving up all my dreams too soon, and not wanting him to think that he could take anything for granted.

'Like what?' he teased.

'Like I might be a teacher,' I said, sticking my chin out defiantly. 'Or I might fly an airplane. Or I might do some singing. Whatever I decide, I'll be too busy to marry you.'

He smiled in a way that suggested he didn't believe for a moment that I would be able to hold out against him for long, and that he could wait, like a cat could wait for a mouse. He didn't let anything I said put him off his mission to charm me and we kept writing to each other after I returned home to England. He was so good-looking that I couldn't get him out of my mind, even though part of me wanted to. I never met anyone else in London who came anywhere close to matching up to David and, as the months passed, I fell further and further in love with the idea of the handsome young man I had seen astride his bike in Kingston. Even when I heard that he had confirmed all my mother's worst predictions and fathered a child with a woman in Jamaica, making me believe that would mean an end to any idle dreams I might have been nursing of us ending up together, I still found myself thinking about him and replying to his letters. Maybe the fact that Dad had had a child with another woman before marrying Mum made the news seem less shocking.

As Noel Coward, who settled in Jamaica at the end of his life, calling it his 'dream island', would have said, I was 'mad about the boy'.

ᗒ CHAPTER NINE ᗕ

A SINGER IN
A BAND

I used to read any music newspapers and magazines I could get hold of, soaking up every bit of knowledge about the business that I could find, and I was always browsing through the small ads, searching out people who were looking for singers who were based in London, preferably close to where we lived. In my head, I could imagine myself replying to one of them, going to an audition and no one taking much notice. I would then see myself climbing up on to the stage and starting to sing, watching everyone doing double takes, stunned by the power and beauty of my voice, begging me to join their bands. (A bit like the 'Susan Boyle moment' on *Britain's Got Talent*.) All these daydreams ended in my becoming a big star.

When you're 14, you can't see any reason why all your dreams shouldn't come true. You haven't yet experienced all the rejection and disappointment that lies in store for anyone who wants to make a career in music. You still have no idea just how many others are out there who share your talents and your dreams and are going to be chasing exactly the same opportunities, maybe even more ferociously than you. You haven't yet met all the people who are going to tell you how brilliant you are and how they are going to make you a star in no time, but who somehow never quite manage to deliver on their promises. You haven't heard all the promises of recording deals that somehow melt away as soon as you feel you are getting within reach of them, like mirages of cool water in the desert. When you're 14, it feels like stardom is only one classified ad away from you, just waiting for you to become old enough to grasp it.

Eventually, I plucked up the courage to take the plunge and respond to an ad which seemed to be offering something that was now within my reach. The advertisers were a group based in Archway, birthplace and childhood home of Rod Stewart and supposed to be the place where Dick Whittington heard the Bow Bells calling him back to become Mayor of London. It's also just up the road from us.

I was still only 15 when I answered their ad and they came to the house to hear me. They were sufficiently impressed to want to hear more and gave me a tape of a song, telling me to learn it and turn up at their studio a few days later. I never had any trouble learning songs.

At the appointed time, I went along to the studio with Mum, trembling with nerves, and sang my heart out for them. They were very nice about it, and they said I was good, but they decided they wanted a 'more mature voice'. The lady they eventually chose to go with was in her twenties and I'm sure that, compared with her, my inexperience on stage must have been obvious. I was disappointed because in my head I had already imagined myself getting the job but, once I had got used to the idea and thought about it more, their positive reaction to me confirmed my belief that all I had to do was wait until I was old enough and then the opportunities would shower down on me. In any case, I knew now that it was possible to get auditions with bands, so I went back home to practise some more with my cassette recorder and to wait for the next opportunity to present itself.

The next ad I found which looked like a possibility appeared about a year later in *Blues and Soul* magazine (this was started in 1966 and the modern version can still be found online). It had been placed by a reggae band based a few miles away in Leytonstone, the area where David Beckham was born and where Damon Albarn from Blur and Jonathan Ross both grew up, as well as the MTV and T4 presenter June Sarpong. The band, called Retro, was led by a drummer who was an experienced professional musician and, even more importantly, knew how to get actual bookings.

At this audition, I sang something that I had written myself, which they liked, and they asked me to join them. I was overjoyed. I felt that I had become a professional musician at last and that it would now only be a matter of time before someone saw me performing with Retro and whisked me off to make a record, which was still my ultimate dream.

Everything about singing with a band was exciting to

me. We used to rehearse at a studio in Hackney and play at college dances and festivals and any other gig that we could get. I was so happy to be performing in front of audiences that never for a moment did I think to ask about payment. I didn't even ask if I could get my travel expenses back. I believe there was a part of me that was frightened I would break the magic spell if I made any sort of demands about anything. I didn't want to risk undoing the good luck that I felt I was enjoying. And I didn't want them to think that I was going to make any sort of trouble for them or be difficult in any way.

Now I have been around a lot longer, I look back and realise that there are thousands of people doing exactly the same thing, keeping the entertainment business alive with their sweated labour and their desperation to perform and record at any cost. They all want the prestige and excitement of being in a band and are frightened that if they ask for money the opportunities being offered to them will melt away. In a way, they're right not to rock the boat because there are a lot of talented singers and performers out there and, if the employers can get someone for nothing, why would they pay? But at the same time every time we give our services away for free we are making it harder for others to make a living. I don't think it is a problem that will ever go away, it's just the way things are, and, because the public now get so much of their music for free from the internet, the problem has become even greater.

People who have never worked in the business sometimes assume that anyone who appears on a stage or a television screen is making a lot of money. In reality, it is often costing them money to be there because of the travel expenses and because they buy their own stage clothes, wanting to look their best in order to make an impression on the audience. At the beginning of our careers, we don't care because we are doing what we love to do more than anything in the world, and because we believe that, if we keep honing our skills and appearing in front of crowds, we will eventually be spotted by someone who has real power and access to real money and that will be the moment when everything changes and the rewards start to pour in.

Sometimes it does happen exactly like that, as it has for Alexandra, and as it happened for Leona Lewis before her and Lena Zavaroni many years before that. The great fear that sets in as the years begin to pass, however, is that you may never be given the chance you need to show people what you can do and that you will never reach a place where you will be able to reap the rewards of all the years of perfecting your skills and knocking on doors, trying to get an opportunity to show the world what you are capable of. That is the fear that keeps everyone striving against the odds for the chance of their moment in the spotlight and stops many performers from being able to earn a fair wage for their skills in the early stages of their careers. If everything goes well for you and you do eventually break through, you can look back on those early experiences as serving an apprenticeship.

But the reality is that there are just too many others trying to get a break, and the law of averages means that most of them will fail to get as far as they hope they will. It's not possible for everyone to make it because there aren't enough hours in the day to listen to and watch them all, even if they are talented. You can see that when you watch the big television talent shows and see what a high standard many of the performers can achieve, even the ones who are sent home early from the shows with nothing.

Evidence of how much these dreams mean to people can be seen most poignantly when you watch the audition process of shows like *The X Factor*, and see the looks of complete desolation that pass over the faces of those who are having their hopes dashed as they realise they are going to go home with the fantasies they have probably been carefully nursing all their lives in shreds and nothing more to look forward to. The ones who will eventually make it to the top, of course, are the ones who refuse to allow any setback to stop them from picking themselves up off the floor and trying again, putting in even more effort than before. If you want to make it, you can never afford to give up trying or hoping, and singing for free if that is all that is being offered.

People who don't have those sorts of dreams find it hard to understand why performers are willing to work so hard for nothing. Even Mum and Dad used to say, 'Shouldn't you be getting paid for this, Melissa?' when they saw how hard I was working.

'No,' I'd dismiss their protests airily, trying to look as if I felt OK about it, as if I understood the business and they didn't, as if I was in possession of some sort of inside knowledge. 'You don't get paid. You just do it.'

Thinking about it, I'm guessing that some of the venues

I appeared at over the years were paying the band leader something for us to be there, although probably not much, but because we weren't asking for anything the band leaders weren't handing any of it on to us. Although it would have been nice to have been paid, it really didn't bother me as long as I could sing to people and as long as I knew they liked what they heard.

The music industry is a really difficult business to make a living in, especially if you love to sing and so never want to turn down any opportunity, but I have to admit that I don't have much of a head for business. Maybe I take after Dad in that way. Looking back now, I know that many of the greatest moments of my life would never have happened if I had demanded to be paid. There are many things which are better than money, and singing is definitely one of them.

I stayed with Retro for a few years until they disbanded. Then, when I was 18, I joined another group, called Impulse, where I came a lot closer to getting a record deal. It all happened by chance, which goes to show how vital it is to keep on singing whenever you are given the opportunity because you never know who is listening or what it might lead to. I had been to a party one Saturday night in Holloway, without telling my parents, needless to say. There was a DJ there with a microphone, who was playing all my favourite songs. I was singing away happily to myself as I danced in a corner of the room when someone in the crowd started shouting. 'There's a girl over there singing, put her on the mic!'

Part of me wanted to run for my life, while another part

couldn't wait to get up there and show them what I could do. The crowd propelled me up on to the stage and the DJ turned the record over to the flip side, which was just the backing track to the A side with the voice removed, like a karaoke version. I strutted my stuff, which everyone seemed to enjoy, and afterwards a guy called Ian, who had told me he was a youth worker, came over to me.

'You're really good, aren't you?' he said.

'Thanks,' I replied, always pleased to receive compliments, even if it was just a chat-up line.

'There's a group up at the youth centre where I work who need a singer,' he went on. 'I'm going to take you up to meet them.'

'OK,' I said, imagining that it would come to nothing, like most of these sorts of promises do.

He was as good as his word and I found myself auditioning for the existing members of Impulse the following Monday night. They were a reggae band but I sang their music in a sort of gospel style, which they had never heard before.

'You're brilliant,' they said. 'Really different.'

I had already worked out that they were proper musicians and when they praised me I felt like I was walking on air. I agreed to join them on the spot. Sometimes you just know when something feels right. There were about seven of us in the band, as there had been in Retro, and we did dozens of gigs together over the following months. We even played at Ronnie Scott's legendary jazz club in Soho's Frith Street. Ronnie had started the club at the end of the 1950s. He was a saxophonist from London who had blown all his savings going to New York when he was 20 and had discovered the jazz scene there, which featured musicians who you could hardly ever hear in Europe. He started the club in Soho initially for British musicians to jam together but then managed to persuade the American Federation of Musicians to allow an exchange deal for American acts and some big stars started to come over to play at his venue. News spreads fast in the music business and it wasn't long before Ronnie Scott's was known as the best jazz club in London.

To be playing somewhere so steeped in music history was fantastic, but still I never thought to ask for any money, because I was just having too good a time. Not that there would have been that much money being handed over anyway. The problem with being in a big group is that even if you do get paid for a gig – say £100 – by the time you have taken out expenses and split it seven ways there really isn't much left.

Anyone going into this business needs to be doing it for the love of music, not for the love of money.

CHAPTER TEN

THE REAL WORLD

I had continued doing well when I moved to my senior school, Starcross Secondary School in Angel, Islington, and my teachers had thought that I would go on to further education. The school had a reciprocal arrangement with Sussex University which allowed for students who were considered to be talented or exceptional in any way to be fast-tracked into provisional university places, pending their A-level results. When the teachers put me on the scheme, Mum and Dad were over the moon and there was a lot of excited talk about my getting a degree and then training to become a teacher.

But when the time came to leave school I decided not to go to university, as had been planned, and I took a job at Marks & Spencer instead, where I had already been working as a Saturday girl and loving it. Maybe it wasn't the best decision, but the thought of spending another three years studying and having no money was too much. I wanted to start earning a living straight away and I wanted to get out into the real world.

I had also looked into becoming an English teacher, because I so enjoyed writing my stories, but everyone told me how badly paid teaching was and that put me off, which suggests I never had a vocation for it in the same way as I had for music. For my music I was willing to work for nothing, but if I was going to be teaching I wanted to be paid a fair salary. It wasn't that I wanted to be rich, just that I was tired of being poor and living in one room. I longed to have a home with a bit of space to walk about, and a bedroom that I didn't have to share all the time. When I was small, I hadn't minded sharing everything because I thought that was how everyone lived, but as I grew older and went to other people's homes I realised that it was possible to expect more from life and I started to crave a bit of privacy and the security of a steady income.

Even though I would never mention it at work, I still harboured a powerful secret dream to be a great singer and sometimes I told myself that I would just work at M&S until I managed to get my big break. I guess if *The X Factor* had been going in those days I would have been one of the thousands of hopefuls who queue up for a chance to audition, just as Alexandra would do more than 20 years later.

Although in some ways I regret not going to university, I do believe that young people need to be allowed to keep their wild dreams for a little while. Having great ambitions is part of the joy of being young and there is plenty of time to be realistic and play safe as you grow older.

I worked at Marks & Spencer's flagship branch in Marble Arch, at the end of bustling Oxford Street, beside

Selfridges. When I first went there for a job interview, I wrote down every question I thought they could possibly ask me, and practised my answers in the mirror as though I was preparing for a performance on stage, so that I would feel confident and completely ready for anything they might throw at me. Never in my life had I talked so eloquently as I did at that interview, and I was offered the job on the spot.

I loved working on the shop floor, partly because I knew I was really good at it, and I loved bringing home a pay cheque each month. It felt so liberating to be able to make a contribution to the costs of things like the groceries and the rent, lifting at least some of the burden that had been on my parents' shoulders for so long, and to no longer have to ask every time I wanted to buy something for myself. But still music and the urge to sing were gnawing away at my soul, and whenever I did gigs at festivals or stood up to sing in a restaurant I knew that was where I really wanted to be. Those were the moments when I felt most fulfilled.

Dealing with the customers at M&S was good for me because it gave me confidence, taught me how to look people in the eye, helped me to make friends and work at the shyness which had always made me hesitate before pushing myself forward. It also exposed me to things that I had been sheltered from because of being kept so much inside the family circle. I had never in my life really come up against colour prejudice before. It simply wasn't something any of us ever thought about or talked about.

I was working one day in the ladies' coats department

when an eccentric upper-class woman demanded some assistance. 'Young lady,' she said, beckoning me over imperiously. 'I'm looking for a winter coat.'

'Of course, madam,' I said, immediately giving her my full attention. 'What colour do you have in mind? We have the season's new colours just in.'

'I'm looking for a particular shade of brown –' she took hold of my hand and rubbed her finger roughly along the skin of my wrist '– in fact, I'm looking for that shade. That's it, nigger brown! Do you have any coats in the shade of nigger brown, my dear?'

I felt like someone had punched me in the face, but I knew I had to maintain a professional demeanour. After all, I was an employee of the prestigious Marks & Spencer plc. I wasn't about to let this racist cow wind me up and make me say something that would lose me my job.

'Of course, madam,' I replied sweetly, as if nothing was wrong. 'I will check with my colleague as I am not quite sure if we do have any coats in the nigger-brown shade.'

'Nigger brown looks like this, I tell you,' she said, pointing to my skin again.

I swiftly passed her over to my white supervisor so that I could go behind the screens and take several deep breaths, reminding myself that I still loved my job and that I needed to stay calm. I was surprised by just how deeply the woman's ignorant words had shocked and wounded me.

On another occasion, it was announced that Mrs Thatcher, the then Prime Minister, was coming to the store to help us celebrate the opening of our new extension. It was going to be a big press and TV event. Remembering what it was like when the Queen came to visit my school, I was highly excited, especially when I was told that I would be in the line-up to shake her hand, and that I would be the one wearing a specially commissioned gold sash with the words 'Marks & Spencer Customer Services – Happy to Help' emblazoned across it.

All the staff from the three floors were briefed and lined up, army style, to greet the Prime Minister. I was the only black member of staff in that particular line-up, as well as the only one wearing a sash, so I was feeling particularly honoured and special.

Mrs Thatcher arrived with all the usual bustle and walked along the line of staff like a queen inspecting her troops, greeting every one individually, chatting for a few moments with them before moving on to the next. As I watched her approach me, with my specially commissioned sash which was intended to catch her attention, I noticed her eyes widen as she looked straight at me for a second. She greeted the person standing beside me on the right and then walked past me, looked back at me again and then shook the hand of the person directly to my left, bypassing me totally. It wasn't as if she didn't see me: she actually looked me straight in the eye as she walked past. I knew I hadn't imagined it because after she had gone everyone was talking about how she had snubbed me by greeting, chatting and shaking the hands of white members of staff while completely ignoring me, the only black one. It seemed a strange and revealing mistake for a politician as clever as her to make.

Despite incidents like that, working at Marks & Spencer

was brilliant. Our diet at home during those years consisted almost solely of M&S foods because each day after work I would have the opportunity to buy cut-price items at staff rates. We filled our fridge and pantry to the brim. I used to buy so much that some days Mum or Dad had to meet me outside work to help me ferry the shopping bags home.

Living in the real, grown-up world felt good, but there was still a part of me that was in love with music, and there were the letters that were still arriving from David in Jamaica, full of plans and promises for the sort of future I could look forward to if I would agree to spend it with him. It's hard when you are young to know which path to follow when you are being pulled in so many different directions and there seem to be so many options open to you. But the decisions you make in those early years, when you are still totally inexperienced, about what jobs to take, what skills to develop, who to marry, where to live and when to have children will affect the whole of the rest of your life. As time goes by, it becomes harder and harder to take advantage of any opportunities that might come your way because other stuff always get in the way.

CHAPTER ELEVEN

AMERICA

I continued to work away at my dreams of success as a singer whenever I could, although I was still uncomfortably reticent about jumping wholeheartedly into 'the big time', giving up my steady salary at M&S and risking everything on getting the big break. If you are going to make it big you have to be prepared to take a few risks and I found that concept hard. I knew how many millions of young girls had dreams of becoming successful singers, and I knew that to the outside world I looked no different from any of them. If I wanted to do it professionally, I had to ensure that the right people got to hear me, but from where I was standing that looked like a full-time job. On the plus side, I was already singing regularly in front of big crowds with the group, which was further than most of the dreamers ever got. There were moments when I felt like I was on the road to fame, most notably when I would come off stage after a good performance and people would tell me how much they had enjoyed it. But the next day I would wake up no further on, and I would know that if I wanted to have any money that week I was going to have to get on the bus and head down to my regular job.

Part of me knew exactly the sort of things I should be doing to push my career forward, while another part of me remained shy and self-conscious. I would sometimes muster enough courage to do something quite daring, like phoning a record company and singing down the phone to the A&R men at the other end. I must have been quite impressive at it because I even got myself a few appointments to be seen that way, but I always chickened out of actually going in to meet the people who could have helped me face to face.

Singing into a phone was one thing, a bit like singing into a tape recorder, or out the window to strangers, but going into a big, shiny record company and performing in front of the professionals where I would be able to see the looks in their eyes was too much for me. What if they were rude about my singing, or about my appearance? What if they were polite but just not interested? If they rejected me, I would find it far harder to keep my dreams alive. We've all seen the looks on the faces of the people who audition for *The X Factor* and have to face the fact that some members of the panel are laughing at them and their foolish ambitions. Terrified of having to go through an ordeal like that, I never found the courage to get to the appointments.

How many people are there out there, I wonder, with beautiful singing voices who just don't have the confidence to push themselves forward and so end up never being heard? Eva Cassidy is a good example of someone who almost slipped through the net. Although she had recorded and released an album, she was still virtually unknown outside her hometown of Washington DC when she died tragically from skin cancer at the age of 33. If it hadn't been for Terry Wogan playing Eva's version of 'Somewhere Over the Rainbow' on his Radio 2 morning show, which unleashed a huge reaction from his listeners, the British public would never have heard this beautiful voice. There was a homemade video of her singing the song which appeared on *Top Of The Pops 2* and since then she has sold something like eight million records and had three number ones. How many others are out there who sing just as beautifully but are never discovered, who die unknown and whose recordings are never picked up by an influential radio producer and given to a disc jockey like Wogan to play?

I don't know if my reluctance to push myself forward was all to do with shyness and fear of rejection, or what it was. I just know I let those chances slip by. Now I simply think I was young and naive and that I missed so many opportunities when they were on offer, but you can't change the way you were in the past. Nowadays, I would never let any opportunity pass me by. We all have to learn from our mistakes.

As long as I didn't stray too far from my own comfort zone, though, I was up for anything. If I was among friends at a party where they had a DJ with a sound system, I would always manage to get hold of the mic and imitate the singers that I loved. People kept telling me I had a great voice and I was feeling confident about that, but I didn't know what I should do in order to make a career of it, or how to find the courage to start approaching the sort of people who could open the right doors for me.

Whenever I could, I was gigging with Impulse, and I loved it, but it didn't look like we were going to be able to move the band on to the next level. We still mainly did festivals for the council in parks, and sometimes we appeared in clubs. The audiences always loved what we did, but there was still no sign of any interest from any record companies.

Mum and Dad used to come to all my gigs to make sure I was safe, and were really encouraging, but I knew there was nothing they could do to help professionally. They knew even less about the music business than I did. When you are completely on the outside of an industry, it often seems impossible that you will ever find a way in. That is why so many thousands of hopefuls grab the opportunities offered by shows like *The X Factor*, where the process for auditioning is obvious for all to see and open to anyone who can get themselves there on the day and fill out a few forms.

One day I was serving a customer in the store when I noticed she was looking at me strangely.

'I know you from somewhere,' she said. 'Do you act?'

'No,' I said bashfully, 'but I do sing.'

'Oh my God,' she shrieked, suddenly really excited. 'I saw you perform in Paradise Park. You were fantastic.'

Her genuine enthusiasm really got to me. Paradise Park is just up the road from where I live, above Pentonville and between the Caledonian and Holloway Roads. It is a world away from where we were now standing in Marble Arch.

The fact that I had made enough of an impact for her to remember and to recognise me in such different surroundings made me think that perhaps I did have a talent that would be worth developing. Maybe, in my own small way, I was beginning to make an impact on the world. At moments like that, I would experience a rush of confidence and feel sure that I would soon get a recording contract, but then the cold light of realism would return once more and I would see that I didn't know what to do next, and that I didn't want to give up my safe, regular income.

At about the same time that Dad came to England with Mum for the first time at the end of the 1950s, his younger brother went to America. He eventually settled in a wealthy area of Long Island in New York, living in a street populated by highly successful Jewish families and enjoying much greater business success than Dad ever achieved. I believe he ran a security company, although I never asked too many questions because I didn't like the way he would boast about his success and put us down for being so hard up and struggling to make a living. No matter how many times we told him, he couldn't understand why we weren't rich and living next door to the Queen or something. He was constantly mocking us for not being as rich as he was. I hated him for the way he talked down to us, telling us we were stupid because we weren't wealthy like him. In my fantasies, I imagined myself becoming a famous singer just so I could show him how wrong he was about us.

I wonder how many of the people who dream of being famous have one or two people in mind who they want to prove themselves to. Becoming rich is one way to show that you aren't the loser that some people say you are, but, however much money you make, there will always be someone who has more, who can still look down on you and find a way to make you feel bad about yourself and your achievements. But if you become a star, surely no one can question the fact that you are a success, or that you have something unique that no one else can beat. Being a star puts you at the very top of the heap. That was how I thought anyway, as I lay in bed at night picturing a scene where my uncle would see me up on stage in front of a huge, cheering crowd, with Mum and Dad looking on proudly.

Dad adored his brother and would never hear anything bad said about him, refusing to believe that my uncle felt any differently about him and choosing not to notice the mocking tone his own brother constantly used towards him. My uncle had had heart trouble, which had affected his kidneys, and I remember Dad saying that he would donate one of his kidneys if it was a match, which was a big thing for him to say. He would have done anything for his brother.

When my uncle rang in 1980 and told Dad he had a business opportunity for him in New York, Dad rushed straight over like a big excited kid. Whatever I might feel about my uncle, I couldn't deny that he was a successful businessman, and we were all very optimistic that this might prove to be a turning point and that we might soon have enough money to actually get ourselves properly established somewhere again instead of constantly having to rent rooms from people and accept favours from friends.

At the time Dad was in New York, Mum and I were living with my sister, Sonia, in Hackney, east London, an area which has been home to a lot of famous cockney characters, including Barbara Windsor, Ray Winstone and Martine McCutcheon. Mum had been staying with friends before that and I had been with Grandma, but she had died and we had to find a room together again. We always seemed to be moving from one place to another and never felt like we had a home that we could call our own. It wasn't that I felt insecure or unhappy, because I always knew I was part of a big, happy, supportive family, but sometimes I craved a little place of my own and a little peace and calm. Sometimes I think perhaps my love of music partly came about because it was an escape route into a world of less complicated thoughts and feelings, a world of stirring beats and heartfelt, clearly expressed emotions.

I never found out any of the details about what happened when Dad got to America, and I didn't like to ask, but I don't think things can have gone too well because he ended up not staying in his brother's big white mansion on Long Island, but was put into a damp, rundown apartment that my uncle owned somewhere in the Bronx. I doubt if there ever actually was a business venture. I think my uncle probably just wanted to have Dad around so he could sneer at him and so he would look good by comparison. Or perhaps he just needed a lowly caretaking job doing at the apartment and thought Dad would be his cheapest option.

Dad confessed to me that he was actually paying rent to his brother for the privilege of being there and that he was also working at two local dry-cleaning firms in order to make ends meet and support himself. I don't know if any of that was part of the 'business opportunity' that my uncle was offering, but I do know that when Dad finally gave up and came back to London he had terrible asthma, which led to him going to hospital for several weeks and developing pneumonia, which I was always sure was caused by the damp conditions of the apartment he had been living in.

Mum and I first heard that he had fallen ill over there when his doctor rang to tell us that he believed Dad needed hospital treatment but that he would never be able to afford it in America. He said that Dad would have to come back to England to get help. When I heard this, I immediately rang Dad and offered to go over and fetch him, but he said we had to save our money and that he could manage the trip on his own. Even when he arrived back in London, with all his dreams of making it in America in ruins, Dad would still never hear a word said against 'me brother'. He still thought everything about him was wonderful. He had been so keen to reconnect with him and share his success with him and it broke my heart to see him used so badly.

I stayed with my uncle in Long Island on a visit once and, despite my feelings about him, I liked the rest of his family a lot, especially his wife, who was lovely to me. The couple's two daughters worked in the finance industry and later had offices in the Twin Towers at the time of the 9/11 attacks, but both were able to escape to safety, being on the lower floors. Their father had died the year before the incident, so he was spared those terrible few hours of anxiety that the rest of us went through before we were able to be sure they had survived.

The reason I was in America in 1981, and able to visit my uncle and his family, was that Mum and Sonia had arranged for me to go and stay with my virtual sister, Beverley, in Miami, to help me to get over the loss of my grandmother.

The moment the plane touched down, I immediately fell in love with America, partly because of the music, which had been allowing me to soak up the culture and history and feel of the country since as long as I could remember. It felt a bit like I was coming home. So many of the records that I had bought over the years had been imports from the States and some of them hardly made any impact in Europe beyond dedicated enthusiasts like me.

This was the period when Debbie Harry was making it big all over the world in Blondie. One of her biggest hits was the old Jamaican reggae song 'The Tide Is High'. I think it was originally written in the 1930s in Kingston by a DJ called Duke Reid, and then rearranged in the 1960s by John Holt, another Jamaican performer who started as a kid entering local talent contests. He sang the song when he was with the Paragons. Also in the charts around that time, Dolly Parton was singing about '9 to 5' and Kim Carnes about 'Bette Davis Eyes'. 'Imagine' and 'Woman' went back to the top of the charts after the assassination of John Lennon in December 1980, and Michael Jackson was singing 'One Day In Your Life'. The Police were enjoying their fourth hit with 'Every Little Thing She Does Is Magic' and Adam Ant, a stylish working-class boy from north London, was riding high with a string of hits.

Whenever I heard something from America I liked being played on a radio station in England, I would have to go to the local record store in Chapel Market to order it. I then always seemed to have to wait ages for the records to be shipped over, which would drive me mad with impatience. But in Miami I could go out and buy the songs as soon as they were released.

Beverley's son, Mark, was like a brother to me and we totally bonded during that trip. He was a really good singer and all we did all day was listen to the radio and watch music videos on MTV. The station was still pretty new then and it felt to me like I had arrived in heaven as I lay in front of the screen letting endless songs and exciting, glossy, highly choreographed images wash over me, imagining that it was me on the screen.

It was a revolutionary moment in pop history. It was like we were now a million light years away from the staid, black-and-white images I had watched of Lena Zavaroni in knee socks, Alice bands and frilly blouses, performing alongside old-fashioned variety acts like comedians and jugglers. Even though there was still controversy over how few black artists were appearing on the station, Michael Jackson was about to release *Thriller*, which would move everything on again, opening the doors for a whole raft of new black performers to become the biggest stars in the world. It felt as if everything was changing for the better, like music might be going to take over the world and I longed to be part of it all.

Mark and I bought dozens of records that I wouldn't have been able to get in Chapel Market and I ended up coming home with my suitcase weighed down with vinyl. He liked to eat too, just like me, and introduced me to Burger King, which had been going in Miami since the 1950s but hadn't yet opened in Britain. I already loved Wimpy and McDonald's and now I had another favourite place to add to the list, with its wonderful 'Whopper'. I noticed there were lots of big people on the beaches and streets of Miami, making me feel quite normal and happy just being myself.

Beverley's house was beautiful and I actually got to have my own bedroom, which felt like paradise. It's hard to explain how luxurious it feels to be able to close a door on the outside world and be totally alone and quiet in a room with your thoughts if you have never been able to do it before. Privacy is a luxury that we all too easily take for granted.

From Miami I flew up to Long Island to stay with my uncle's family, spending a happy day acting the tourist in Manhattan, going from one famous sight to another while my cousins were at work in the World Trade Center. I gazed down on the city from the top of the Statue of Liberty and strolled in Central Park, close to where Lennon had been shot, living the dream and feeling excited by all the possibilities that might lie ahead for me. I think the buzz and excitement of Manhattan has that effect on a lot of people, making anything seem possible

CHAPTER TWELVE

MY LITTLE CARIBBEAN WEDDING

For seven years, David and I had been exchanging letters and declarations of love and I had been thinking about him a lot, wondering if he might be the one for me even though he had had a child by another woman, which was something I had got used to over the years. I suppose all young girls try to imagine what it would be like to be married, and, if there is a charming, handsome boy who keeps on talking like it is a foregone conclusion, the idea is bound to seep into your subconscious eventually.

Although I didn't believe in sex outside marriage, I knew enough about West Indian culture to be aware that he was not unusual in having been unable to keep himself pure until he took a wife. I realised that if I turned down every man who wasn't a virgin I was going to be very short of potential suitors. That knowledge, however, did not quite quell the voices of warning that were nagging away at the back of my mind.

David kept telling me he wanted to marry me and I

certainly hadn't met any other boys in that time who I had liked better or thought were more attractive. Because of my very firm beliefs about morality, I still didn't want to sleep with any man unless I was married to him, so the memory of David was growing increasingly potent as the years passed and my thoughts naturally turned to the personal aspects of my future.

In 1984, when I was 20, I went for a holiday with a friend to the Bahamas, and I added Jamaica to my itinerary without telling Mum and Dad. It wasn't that I wanted to deceive them, but more that I didn't really know for sure in my own mind why I was doing this and so I didn't want to have to try to explain it to anyone else, especially someone who was bound to worry about me and want to know what I was thinking. I had a feeling Dad might do a lot of shouting if he knew I was going to see David. My boss very kindly said that I could have six weeks' leave for the trip.

This was the year when Madonna released her first number-one album, *Like a Virgin*, Stevie Wonder was singing 'I Just Called to Say I Love You' and Tina Turner wanted to know 'What's Love Got to Do With It?' Lionel Richie was singing 'Stuck on You' and 'All Night Long' and Billy Joel was having a hit with 'Uptown Girl'.

By now, Mum and I had been given a beautiful two-bedroom flat by Islington Council, and we had finally managed to afford a colour television of our own. It was beginning to feel like life was becoming good at last. But at the same time Dad had decided to get his own place because he said he needed his 'own space'. I have to admit

Mum never did seem able to resist nagging him and he probably did need to escape from the sound of her voice for at least a few hours a day. Despite having a home of his own, he was round at our place more than he was at his own, helping me to care for Mum as she became sicker from the diabetes and kidney failure. They were never officially separated and life never seemed that different as far as I was concerned; they had just come to an arrangement that seemed to suit them both. Around this time Dad bought himself a gross yellow Cortina, which he was fantastically proud of but which probably suggested he was having some sort of mid-life crisis.

Like so many West Indian men, Dad was a bit of a philanderer, and a lot of women found him very attractive, despite the fact that he was only five feet tall, but he was always discreet about it and never flaunted his girlfriends in Mum's face like some of the men we knew. I think she must have known a bit of what he was up to but she seemed to be content to have a home and a child and enough money to live and she pretty much allowed him do what he pleased. Maybe she was just becoming too exhausted to care any more as her body grew weaker.

As she became progressively less able to cope, Dad would come round when I was at work and do all the cooking and cleaning and running round for her. He never complained about any of it. He knew he had vowed to be there for her 'for better or for worse' and when things got bad he honoured that vow completely.

Even though I was earning a steady wage, money was still very tight when it came to paying for luxuries and it took me months to pay off the air fare to the Bahamas. Each week I would go into the British Airways office opposite my workplace, after the wages had been paid, to hand over a little more. The staff on the counter got to know me well, greeting me by name each time I came in, encouraging me as I worked slowly and steadily towards my target.

David wrote to tell me how much he was looking forward to me arriving in Jamaica and I grew increasingly excited at the prospect of seeing him again, although I was still unsure how I would react when he was actually standing in front of me. I had kept every letter he had ever written to me over the years of our separation, and took the whole bundle with me in my suitcase, including the envelopes they had arrived in, even though I still hadn't made a conscious decision about whether I was going to give in and agree to marry him or not. Just the thought of seeing him again was making my heart beat a little faster.

When I arrived in Kingston and saw him again, I was instantly bowled over. He was even more handsome and charming than I remembered. Now he was a fully grown man, with all the confidence that comes with it. If he had been easily able to sweep me off my feet when he was a teenager, he had even less trouble now. From the moment I landed, we were together almost every minute of the day, even though I was staying with my aunt, and it felt like the years we had been apart had never happened. We were completely relaxed and comfortable together, laughing at the same things, talking all the time.

It was his aunt, who was a district JP and a highly

respected woman, who put into words what a lot of people must have been thinking as they watched us together.

'You know, Mel,' she said when she and I were alone one day, 'you and David should get married. You make a perfect couple.'

'I don't want to marry someone who already has a child,' I said doubtfully. 'I want any children we have to be our first.'

I had been telling David the same thing each time he asked me again to marry him, but I think by that stage I was just using it as an excuse to buy myself some more time. Perhaps I was just nervous about making such a huge commitment, frightened that I might be letting my heart run away with my head, while at the same time being deeply tempted to give in and agree to his constant stream of proposals. He kept begging me to give him another chance, and each time he told me how much he loved me my resolve was worn down a little further.

'I made one mistake,' he would say, 'but don't let that come between us. I was just a kid and you were so far away for so many years.'

He was so persuasive, the tropical evenings were so romantic and his aunt was so encouraging I was finding it harder and harder to think of any sensible reason to say no. After all, both Mum and Dad had had children from previous relationships when they met, and they had still managed to have a pretty good marriage, even if they were now living separately. His aunt even promised to make all the arrangements for the ceremony so that I would have nothing to worry about. Eventually, they wore me down and I gave in, put aside my last lingering doubts and agreed.

It was never going to be a big wedding at such short notice, but David's aunt did manage to get me a veil for the ceremony, which was to be held in the little local church, and she recruited two witnesses from somewhere to make the whole thing legal. There were no other guests, not even my aunt, who I was staying with, as everything was organised so quickly.

I wore a white beach dress from Marks & Spencer, which I had brought with me for the holiday, and the final effect with the veil was actually quite good. David wore a white cotton shirt and tie with black trousers, but no jacket because of the heat, and looked as cool as always.

Deep at the back of my mind, a little voice continued to question why I was doing this, even as I stood in front of the priest and repeated my vows in a sort of daze, but I seemed to be being swept along by the momentum of the whole thing and by everyone else's enthusiasm. I told myself that all young brides probably got nervous when they took such a momentous step. It was only to be expected, especially when I was so far away from Mum and Dad and my close friends and family.

People always like to see young couples being paired off. It must appeal to something very deep and instinctive in all of us, a bit like the way seeing a small baby makes almost any woman feel maternal pangs. I told myself not to take any notice of the uncomfortable little voice, that everyone probably had some doubts and that, as long as it was all legal and properly done, it would be OK. I told myself to just enjoy the day for what it was – my 'big day' – and then take life as it came.

Even as a small girl, I'd never cherished any great dreams about being given a big romantic wedding anyway because I knew they cost a lot of money and would always be beyond my reach. Thinking back now, I guess that David's family was keen to get the ceremony over as quickly as possible so that we could start the process of getting him out of Jamaica and over to England. They believed that he was always in danger of becoming a target as long as he was on the island because of the way he dressed and the fact that it was obvious he was successful and had money.

From my own experience as a schoolgirl in Kingston, I knew that their fears were not without reason. When you live in a community with so much poverty, there is bound to be envy directed towards anyone who seems to have more. The town was also becoming increasingly notorious for its violent crime and many middle-class homes were beginning to resemble fortresses as people tried to protect themselves and their possessions. It is a problem that has never gone away and in 2005 Jamaica gained the sad distinction of having the highest murder rate in the world, although it has since been overtaken by trouble spots like Iraq and Sierra Leone.

David's mother was American, which was probably why the family had a nice house in the first place, but he was also earning a good living himself. Not only was he a welder by trade, he also ran a nightclub with his stepfather and was never short of money. His family must have believed that someone who worked as hard as he did would do better in a country like England than he could ever hope to do in Jamaica and I'm sure they were right about that. It was the same mixture of hope and ambition that had first lured Dad into leaving the place in 1958. I'm not saying that David's family meant to do me any harm, or even that they were using me as his ticket off the island, because it must have been obvious to everyone that we were besotted with each other. But I think that must have been why his aunt was so keen for the marriage to be finalised quickly, while I was still in the country. Had I been allowed to go home and 'think about it' some more, who knows how long it would have been before I plucked up the courage to make such a huge decision? If I had done that, my life would have turned out very differently.

As soon as it was all over and the excitement was dying down, I felt an even stronger stab of anxiety than the rumble of disquiet I had experienced during the ceremony. Had I made a terrible mistake? Had I allowed myself to be stampeded into something without thinking it through? Had I allowed things to go too fast? Should I have contacted Mum and Dad to let them know what was happening, even though there would have been no way we could have got them to Jamaica in time for the ceremony? How would they react when I told them? I didn't fancy being on the receiving end of one of Dad's tirades at a time when I was feeling so unsure of things myself. I wanted them to love David as much as I did and I didn't want to have to listen to them putting him down and telling me what a bad husband he was going to be. All these thoughts, and more, were rushing around in my head at the same time.

Partly it felt very grown up to have made such a decision on my own and to now have a husband, but part of me still felt like a naughty schoolgirl who had done something silly and was now going to have to own up to her parents and face the music.

Plucking up all my courage, I phoned Mum to tell her the news. Considering what a bombshell it must have been for her, she was surprisingly calm, which was a relief, although she was not exactly effusive.

'I'm not telling your dad,' she said. 'You can come home and tell him yourself.'

I could understand her reticence and I could hardly blame her. Why should she have to listen to all the shouting he was bound to dish out when he heard the news? None of it was her fault.

The mother of David's child was very upset to hear that he had married a woman from England, believing that it meant he was planning to leave Jamaica and abandon his son, which he pretty much was, and would do again once we had children of our own, although I wasn't to know that then. At that moment, I didn't see things from her point of view at all and I thought she was being unfair to David, not allowing him the chance to make a life for himself, holding him back because of one mistake he had made in the past, when he was still little more than a boy. Now his son from that relationship lives in London too, quite close to us, and we get on well, but at the time it all seemed so complicated and a terrible emotional minefield. When you are 20 years old, everything seems so much more dramatic and threatening, and you don't realise what a mellowing effect the passing years will have on everyone and everything. When I look at Alex up on the screen, I can see how emotional and vulnerable she still is, and I remember that she is the same age I was when I took the massive step of marrying her father, just a few years away from being a child. I can hardly believe it.

Although Mum was being cool about it now that I was presenting her with a 'done deed', and would always make an effort to get on with him, she was never a fan of David's. Right from the start, she had always warned me against him.

'All West Indian men are the same,' she would say. 'They all make bad husbands and fathers. They all play around and leave their women to do all the work of bringing up the kids.'

I guess one of the reasons that I didn't tell her when things started to go wrong between David and me in the years to come was because I was proud and never wanted to admit to her that she had been right and I had made a mistake when I acted so impulsively on that holiday and came home married. David was so impossible for me to resist. I believed every line that he spun me about how he would always be faithful and always look after me and never betray me, because I wanted so much for it all to be true. He could always be very convincing when he wanted. At one stage he considered becoming a preacher, and he would have been very good at it too because he had the charisma that is required to win over a congregation, but he lacked the dedication to become a man of God. David liked women too much and they would eventually be his downfall.

Although I hadn't planned to marry him when I packed David's letters into my suitcase before leaving England, having them with me made it possible for me to prove to the authorities at the British Embassy that our love match was genuine and that David wasn't just marrying me to get a ticket to Britain. So maybe when I was planning my trip it was already in my mind that something might happen once I was with him. Perhaps it was inevitable that we would end up together and I was just playing out my destiny.

Once the official at the embassy had looked through the letters, and had seen how much history we had together, he didn't hesitate to give David the permission he needed to move to London with me so that we could start our married life together. I had left London as a young working girl going on holiday with a girlfriend and I returned a couple of weeks later as a married woman, although not yet accompanied by my new husband. My whole life was about to change.

CHAPTER THIRTEEN

MY BABIES

I returned to England before David because it was the end of my holiday and I needed to get back to my job, and he followed a couple of months later, once he had sorted out his affairs in Kingston and was ready to start his married life in a new country. It was going to be a big step for him as well as for me.

Initially, we had no choice other than to live with Mum in her two-bedroom council flat in Archway. I was really nervous about how she and David would get on under such close conditions, but she accepted him completely as my husband and never said anything more against him. Now that we were legally married, I suppose there was nothing much she could do other than hope for the best. Mum had been through a lot in her life and she had learned that sometimes you just have to resign yourself to the way things are, unless you want to be fighting people all the time. If you come from a country as hot as Jamaica, you learn not to work yourself up into a sweat about anything you don't have to, and anyway by that stage her energy levels must have been almost running out because of what was happening inside her. I was so grateful to her for being so understanding and accepting.

Perhaps she felt that David had matured into a good potential husband since she had last seen him. For better or worse he was now part of the family and she was wise enough to know that it would be better if we all got along peacefully. She gave no indication of what she might truly be feeling, making him feel welcome in the house, buying him clothes and generally looking after him like a mother-in-law should. Starting our married life in her home was never going to be ideal, but it was better than being homeless and it gave us a chance to catch our breath and to try to work out what to do next.

I always meant to hold another wedding ceremony once we had arrived back in London, so that we could include all the family, but we never did get round to that because our lives were so busy and money was so short, and then I fell pregnant almost as soon as David arrived. It was my fault it happened so quickly because I hadn't been taking any precautions. The reason I had been so casual about the whole thing was that I'd never had periods as a girl and I thought I couldn't get pregnant.

I never did find out why my periods hadn't started at the same time as everyone else's but maybe it was something to do with my weight, or perhaps all the years that I had felt isolated and alone, without many friends, had had a bad effect on my system. Or maybe it was something to do with my body reacting to the lack of privacy in my life. Who knows? All I do know is that it was a major shock to find I was pregnant, although I was really happy to discover that I was going to be able to have kids after all, once I had got used to the idea. I loved my handsome, charming husband and I couldn't think of anything better than starting a family with him.

Once there was a baby on the way, Mum had to officially kick us out of her house and make us homeless in order for the council to agree to give us a flat of our own. The thought of trying to fit a new baby into the existing accommodation was a bit too much for all of us. David and I needed some space of our own to start our little family. After a short stay with Dad, who was also being very laidback about the surprise addition of David and a new baby to the family, the council found us a two-bedroom flat in a large grey concrete block above the Argos store in Old Street, just along from the tube station, on the edge of Shoreditch, an area which in the past had theatres and music halls and a lively atmosphere and in the last ten years has become fashionable all over again, with bars, restaurants and clubs springing up everywhere. We couldn't believe our luck. Two bedrooms! That meant we wouldn't even have to share with the baby.

I felt like I had finally come of age, with a home of my own, a husband to share my life with and a baby on the way, not having any idea that this would be where all the problems would soon start between us.

To start with, independence was a good feeling, one that I had never experienced fully before. David got a job working in an ice-cream factory and I was still at M&S, so

I thought it wouldn't be long before any money troubles became a thing of the past and we would be able to give our first baby, and any others that might follow, a great start in life.

What I didn't realise was that when David was out of my sight he was meeting and chatting up other women. I guess they were as attracted to him as I had been the first time I saw him standing in the street in Kingston with his mate, so he never had any difficulty getting their attention. I now know that he was incapable of resisting any temptation that might be put in his way, but at the time I knew nothing about any of this and in my blissful ignorance I was happily preparing myself for the adventure of motherhood and nest-building.

I don't know where I got the idea that when you are pregnant you need to eat twice as much food, but I truly did believe it. I told myself that I needed to eat more in order to nourish the baby growing inside me, that it was my duty to gorge myself endlessly on anything and everything that I could get my hands on, and nobody bothered to explain any different to me. Or, if anyone was saying anything, I certainly wasn't listening. All my life Dad and Mum had encouraged me to eat, to make food my friend, to comfort myself by filling my stomach way beyond anything I needed in order to be healthy, so why would I stop now, when I had the perfect excuse? David never complained either, although I have no way of knowing now what he might have been thinking privately.

Believe it or not, I put on eight stone during the pregnancy, which is basically equivalent to the weight of a small adult rather than a small baby. I also developed gestational diabetes, just like Mum had done when she was carrying me. I guess there must have been a propensity for the condition lurking in my DNA, but I certainly didn't help myself with all my trips to burger bars and pick-'n'-mix counters.

Mum and Dad and David might not have said anything, but the doctors overseeing the pregnancy soon became concerned as I ballooned up before their eyes and they instructed me to take two months' bed rest at the Whittington Hospital (named after Dick Whittington, the area's favourite son), the same place where I had been born 21 years earlier. But that meant I was taking even less exercise and being in hospital had no effect on my eating because I simply rallied Mum and Dad to bring food in to me in order to supplement the hospital meals. The fact that I was safely out of the way also meant that I had even less of an idea what David might be getting up to.

As my weight continued to increase, the doctors became more and more alarmed. They decided to bring forward the birth because the baby was growing inside me at the rate of 1lb a week and they estimated that if they left her to go full term she would be 13lb by the time she arrived, almost as much as I was when I was born. So Sheniece made her appearance three weeks early, via Caesarean section, and even then she still weighed in at 10lb. I guess we are all programmed to repeat the mistakes of our parents, unless we are educated differently.

Sheniece was the fattest, hairiest, greediest baby I have ever come across. She even had downy hair on her ears, like a little werewolf, and she seemed to have inherited my appetite from day one, taking double quantities of milk all through the day and sometimes at night as well. To me at the time, however, in my state of deluded new motherhood, she seemed the most beautiful creature I had ever seen. I was besotted with my baby and spent every minute of the day doting over her.

After the birth, I made no effort to lose any weight. I didn't even think about it. So by the time I went back to work, when Sheniece was seven months old and I was happy to leave her with Mum, I had shed only two stone of the eight I had gained. Once I was venturing back outside the home, it was embarrassing to be so big, I have to admit, and I knew it was all my own fault, but still I chose to do nothing about it, preferring the comfort of eating to the comfort of not being overweight.

Although I still loved my job and I was happy to be back among my friends, I would have much preferred to stay home with my baby if we could have afforded it, but, although David was working full-time, he didn't seem to be contributing any money to the household budget. I couldn't work out what he was spending his wages on and whenever I brought up the subject he always seemed to be able to come up with some story which sounded convincing at the time. It was dawning on me that I was going to have to continue to work to support Sheniece and me and to ensure that we kept a roof over our heads. I was beginning to realise that I was never going to be able to rely on David to support us and take care of us, which was disappointing, but not the end of the world because I was confident I was capable of earning a reasonable living by myself.

In fact, I knew plenty of families where the woman earned all the money as well as doing all the housework and I also knew lots of women who were having to bring up families without any man around at all. I didn't want to nag at David and risk having him walk out on me completely. What woman would choose to drive the father of her child away if she doesn't have to? I'm sure there are plenty of women around who have fallen into that trap in the past and plenty more who will continue to do so in the future.

By the time I went back to work at M&S, however, I was already pregnant again. Although I was happy overall, there were times, lying awake in the middle of the night staring at the ceiling, waiting for David to come home, when I wasn't sure how I would be able to cope with another baby when I was only just finding my feet in the real world again. Mum and Dad were totally supportive and promised to help in any way they could and I knew they meant it because over the years I had seen Mum help dozens of other young women to look after their children, and I knew that, for all his funny ways, Dad could always be relied upon to help whenever he could. But I also knew that Mum's health was failing badly and that it would be unfair to expect too much of her. I don't know how young mothers manage if they haven't got the full support of their families behind them and I have always aimed to be as helpful to my children as Mum and Dad were to me in those difficult times.

Although I didn't make the same mistake with the overeating during the second pregnancy, David Junior was also born by Caesarean section and weighed a sturdy 10lb on delivery. The women in our family very seldom gave birth to boys, so his arrival was the cause of much celebration. Mum and Dad always liked to celebrate things and they were never short of friends who were happy to join them for a party. David was the moaniest of babies, crying all the time for no apparent reason, but Mum was still happy to take on responsibility for him as well as Sheniece when the time came for me to go back to work once again.

Inevitably, there were the usual problems you get when another child arrives. One time when David was still a baby, I saw that he was sucking on something in his cot. When I put my fingers in his mouth, I found that Sheniece had inserted one of her Love Hearts sweets. Maybe it was a kind gesture, or maybe she was hoping to choke him. She certainly used to bully him a lot when she was tiny. I was pushing them both in a double pushchair one day, distracted by whatever I was doing, when a passing woman stopped me.

'Have you seen what's going on in there?' she asked.

Peering round the hood, I found Sheniece practically on top of her baby brother, beating him up.

Sheniece, when she was little, was so greedy she would eat anything she could get her hands on. One time when I was busy doing something else, she went into the bathroom with David in tow. She climbed on the toilet, opened the medicine cabinet and found a bar of laxative chocolate. By the time I came looking for them, the chocolate was all round their mouths and the wrapper was discarded on the floor. I immediately panicked and called an ambulance. They were rushed to hospital to have their stomachs pumped, although as it turned out David had only been allowed the tiniest bit while Sheniece had swallowed virtually the whole bar and ended up having to spend two nights in hospital.

By the end of the year when David Junior was born, I discovered that I was pregnant yet again. It was hard to imagine how I had ever believed I was going to end up childless. It seemed David only had to look at me and I would conceive and I was beginning to feel like I was on a production line.

I was happy at the thought of having another baby because I loved Sheniece and little David beyond all reason, but how were we going to cope with three babies under four years of age? Could I really expect Mum to look after three of them at her age, especially given the state of her health? But did I have any other choice? If I stayed home, could we exist without my salary coming in?

David didn't seem bothered about anything to do with us any more. He was always staying out and telling me that it was because he was working late, but he still didn't bring any money into the house. I could tell he was distracted by something and whenever he was there we argued all the time. I still loved him as much as I always had but it was just so hard to manage when it felt like I was having to shoulder all the responsibilities of the household myself. This, I thought, was what Mum had meant when she warned me against marrying a West Indian man, but I didn't want to give her any idea that she had been right and that I had made a mistake. I wanted her to believe that David was different from the others, that he was a good husband, so I said nothing. But it's hard work living a lie.

'You are too close to your mother, girl,' David would scoff if I ever mentioned something she had said. 'You need to cut the reins!'

Maybe he had a point, but how could we possibly have managed without her constant help and support? She did a darn sight more for me than he ever did. If he had ever issued an ultimatum of 'Either your mother goes, or I go', I would always have chosen her over him. I was beginning to become very angry about the way my life was going. This wasn't how things were meant to be. Where was the music in my life now? How come everything I loved, everything that made life worth living, was slipping away? Why did everything have to be such a struggle?

Alexandra, my third child, was born in August 1988. She was another 10lb Caesarean production, but this time I had managed to produce a baby that was both pretty and contented. She was slightly jaundiced at birth and had to be put under special ultraviolet lights for a while. It upset me at the time to see her like that because I didn't understand what was going on, but the treatment worked and she was able to come home ten days after her arrival in the world.

Motherhood is a wonderful experience, possibly the best in the world, but it doesn't leave much room for anything else. How many girls start out with wonderful dreams of becoming singers or musicians, actresses or models, fashion designers or photographers, lawyers or entrepreneurs, and end up too exhausted from the efforts of running homes and families to be able to achieve anything else? Nothing had changed inside me since the moment when I first watched Lena Zavaroni and longed to be where she was, but all around me everything else had changed.

Everything was changing for Lena as well of course. When she was 13 and attending the Italia Conti, she became anorexic and her weight dropped right down to four stone. Pictures in the press showed her looking like a skeleton and who knows what pressures she felt she was under after becoming a household name so young. She went on to marry a computer consultant but the marriage didn't work and they separated within a year or two. Although I have certainly never had a problem with being too thin, I guess I had problems with weight and eating too, just like her. Those problems would eventually come close to killing me, just as they eventually led to Lena dying at just 35, after being admitted to hospital for help with her depression.

How could a child who was so full of life and joy, as she had appeared to be on those shows when she was ten years old, have ended up depressed? How could the reality of her life behind the screen have turned out to be so different from the image she projected when she was on it? Her talent brought her everything any stage-struck little girl could ever believe she wanted, but she ended up dying because it all made her so miserable.

Looking back at my own children, it's clear that Alex was always Mummy's little girl, telling me everything that her brothers and sister were up to, which used to drive the others mad. She was never underhand about it, she used to come right out and tell me if she had heard that Sheniece had been smoking or if someone had nicked a biscuit. She used to tell her granddad everything as well, but she would try to boss him around as well, making him cut down his drinking. If she saw him bringing cans of Special Brew into the house, she would follow him around to see where he had hidden them, collect them up as soon as his back was turned and re-hide them. For some reason, he never got cross with her.

'It's not good for you to drink, Granddad,' she would say.

'Please, Putto,' he would plead, 'just give me the beer and then we can talk.'

He used to have nonsensical nicknames for all of us and they always started with the letter 'p'. Mine was 'Plang' for some reason I never worked out.

David was always the most serious one in the family, very bright at school and very hard-working. He did brilliantly in his exams and went on to university to study accounting and European business. He's always the cool, calm voice of reason when everyone else is being dramatic and shouting at the top of their voice, like a judge pondering every situation. He's the one that Alex trusts now to help her with her finances. Everyone trusts David.

Alex has always been brilliant at looking after her money. I used to give her £1 a day for her school bus fare, but she would walk instead and save the money, putting it in the bank until eventually she had saved up £600.

And Sheniece was and still is the most volatile of all of us. When something upsets her, she doesn't try to hide it and will shout at the top of her voice whatever the time of night, which can be annoying for the neighbours.

Back when they were still kids, even though my days were filled to bursting with the responsibilities of holding down a job and looking after them and David, I still knew deep in my heart that I wanted to sing. The problem was I still didn't have any idea how to build a career. I didn't understand the business like I do now and I didn't have the same guidance that Alexandra would be able to get when it came to her turn. Part of me didn't care about that side of it because I didn't want to be famous particularly: I just wanted to perform and to get my voice on vinyl. I had never forgotten how right it felt when I was using my voice to make music, nor the enormous glow of joy I had felt whenever anyone had praised me or been surprised to discover what I was able to do. I wanted to be able to hear my voice coming out of the radio, and for Mum to be able to hear it, along with everyone else that I knew. I was like a junkie, longing for a fix of performing, something that had once given me the greatest highs of my life.

That year George Michael released 'Kissing a Fool' from his *Faith* album and Elton John was singing 'Candle in the Wind', but the track which was being voted song and record of the year was 'Don't Worry, Be Happy' by Bobby McFerrin, which could have been my husband's theme tune. It was part of the soundtrack for the film *Cocktail*, which had Tom Cruise escaping from the rat race of New York, working as a bartender in Jamaica and falling in love. The film won two 'Golden Raspberry' awards for 'worst film' and 'worst screenplay' and Tom Cruise was nominated for 'worst actor', but lost to Sylvester Stallone for his performance in *Rambo III*.

'Don't worry, be happy' is wonderful advice, but sometimes it just isn't possible. There was a pressure building up inside me which was bound to burst out sooner or later.

CHAPTER FOURTEEN

BACK ON STAGE

Perhaps if David had been more discreet about his affairs I would have been able to keep going with the whole pretence, telling myself that everything was all right and just keeping myself busy with the children and ignoring all the obvious clues to what was really going on. After all, that's just what so many wives of unfaithful husbands do. But he started a relationship with a girl who decided she wanted him all for herself.

She instigated a campaign of harassment against me, calling our number and making threats, telling me to get out of David's life and leave him to her. It was obvious from what she was saying that he had been with her in our home and that she knew everything about our lives as a family, which felt deeply threatening. No woman likes to think that an interloper has managed to get inside her nest, into the home where she tries to keep her babies safe.

Although the discovery that David had betrayed me shattered my heart, I didn't let her know it. I fought back with all the cunning I could muster, even though my spirit was broken. The more I told her that she would never split us up, that she would never be able to have David, the more threatening she became. I even tried becoming her friend and confidante, convincing her for a while that he was betraying us both and that we should work together to defeat him. But it didn't work for long and her threats became more and more violent. For the sake of the children, I knew I had to get out of the house. It seemed that there was a very real danger she would do something that might harm them as well as me. I went to the housing association we were renting our home from and they agreed to move us to a safe address a few miles away, an address she would know nothing about.

Obviously shocked by the amount of disruption his mistress was causing to his life, David kept promising me that the affair was all over and that it had been a mistake and that he had learned his lesson, but now that I was alerted to what had been happening under my nose I could see that he had no real intention of changing his ways. In fact, I wonder if he was even capable of it. I expect he was telling the other woman the exact opposite story to the one he was telling me, assuring her that his marriage was over and it would only be a matter of time before he was rid of me. When talking to me, he claimed that he didn't want to lose me and the children, but it was becoming obvious he wasn't planning to give up on any of his other pleasures either.

As well as being hurt myself, and angry because I felt his behaviour was harming the children, I was puzzled too because it would never have occurred to me to be unfaithful to my partner. I simply didn't understand it. I still didn't even believe in sex outside marriage between single people. In fact, I never have changed my opinion on that one, although I have had to accept that most people feel differently from me. The continued betrayals left me feeling very vulnerable, but I knew I had to be strong and keep going for the sake of the kids and the rest of the family.

I finally had to admit to Mum and Dad that the whole marriage had been a terrible mistake, that they had been right about him all along. I knew that, along with the kids, Mum and Dad were my anchors in life and I realised, now the scales had fallen from my eyes, that I couldn't go on with the pretence. I couldn't just look the other way and tell myself it wasn't happening. I was going to have to end the marriage for all our sakes.

Splitting up with David wasn't as great a sacrifice as it might have been because he had never been any help to me around the home anyway and he had never offered any financial support. When I told him to go, that I could manage for myself, I knew Mum and Dad would be there for me in any way they could and having that sort of support makes you strong enough to face anything. David tried to change my mind but by that stage I was adamant. Knowing that he had betrayed me so completely, I didn't believe I would ever be able to trust him again.

Eventually, he realised I was serious and he went. I heard that he was still with the other woman and that he had made her pregnant as well. From the moment he left our house, he didn't try to do anything to help support any of our children. He didn't even bother to contact them direct to find out how they were doing at school or just to say 'hi'. In some ways, I felt like a great weight had been lifted from my shoulders and I could get on with my life without having to think about him, but in my heart I felt alone and desperately sad and disappointed at the way things had turned out. I adore my kids more than anything in the world, but never in a hundred years had I imagined that I would end up as a single mother, struggling through each day, trying to keep everything together.

So many of the West Indian men I have met behave in a similar way towards women. They talk about being 'on the game', which basically means seeing how many women they can reel in, use and then chuck back. If ever they are caught out, they just deny everything, no matter how blatant the evidence is against them. The singer-songwriter Shaggy comes from Jamaica and he knew exactly what he was talking about when he wrote his hit 'It Wasn't Me', which came out a couple of years later.

They all seem to believe that they have to have as many women as possible on the go at the same time but they don't seem to think that they have any responsibility for supporting or looking after the children that they produce as a result. I have tried to break that cycle with my sons because I think it is so important that children should have the stability of one mother and one father and that the burden which falls on the shoulders of the mothers who are left to do everything by themselves is often impossible to bear. If I hadn't had my parents there to help, which many young girls don't have, I don't know what would have happened. I have tried to convince the girls that they shouldn't have children until they are married and are as sure as they can be that they have a man who will stay with them. And I pray that they will find good men who will shoulder their responsibilities.

'If you aren't going to be faithful to someone,' I tell the boys, 'then don't commit. If you want to play the field while you are young and single, that's one thing, but only commit to a relationship and to children when you are ready to stay with one person and to take on the responsibilities.'

Because they don't like the way their father has treated us all and they have seen how hard I have had to struggle to keep our heads above water, they agree with me, although I'm sure they get tired of hearing me say the same thing all the time.

An elderly lady I knew had bought herself a Yorkshire terrier puppy, without realising how much exercise and attention he would need once he grew up. He was running rings around her and she asked me if I would like to take him off her hands since she could see how taken I was with him. I still had fond memories of Whitey and Fluffy out in Kingston, and of my cats when I was young. I hadn't had time to think about pets in recent years but now that the idea had been seeded in my head it seemed to me that a dog around the house would be a better bet than a man, and it would be something nice for the kids as well. I agreed to add him to our family.

His name was Barney and he immediately became my best friend and constant companion through those sad but busy times. He went on holiday with me, and slept in the bed with me. I never wanted to be parted from him. When he passed away at just six years old, I think I was even more heartbroken than I had been when I found out about David and the other women.

Barney died of kidney failure, which is interesting because there's a belief in Jamaican folklore that you need to have pets around you because, if you have an illness that is likely to kill you later, the animal will draw the sickness away from you, bearing the consequences on your behalf. If that's true, then poor little Barney had to die so that I could survive when my own kidneys failed a few years later. Maybe it is because of his ultimate sacrifice that I am able to lie here on the dialysis machine and tell you my story. If so, he was an even better friend to me than I imagined at the time.

Once we got Barney, we wanted to have more pets and we already had two other dogs by the time he died, sweet-natured mongrels called Patch and Spice, who are constantly clattering around the house, pushing their noses into the hands of anyone who is willing to pay them the slightest bit of attention. They are also 'a couple' and have managed to produce 25 puppies over the last two years or so, all of which have had to have homes found for them. In the end, I had to accept that Spice was going to need an operation in order to stop the puppy assembly line. Personally, I would have liked to keep every one of them, but the house is already overflowing with people most days, and every bed and couch is occupied most nights, sometimes with a few more people stretched out on the floor. And I could see that adding even more dogs to the mix would be a nightmare. Sometimes you have to make tough choices.

All through the hectic years of raising three small children, I had no time to do anything about my singing and I missed it terribly. I hardly even had time to listen to music. When you already have the voices of children all around you, clamouring for attention, not to mention all the other adults in my life, having a radio babbling in the background as well would probably have been the straw that broke the camel's back. When you are young and without responsibilities, the days are long, with empty hours which you can fill with the things that excite you and stimulate your imagination and your dreams. As the responsibilities and worries of adulthood start to mount up, the hours begin to vanish and before you have time to do any of the things that once used to fill your time and your thoughts it is already the end of the day and you are collapsing into bed exhausted, needing a few hours' sleep before you have to get up and start all over again. You certainly don't feel like going out to parties or clubs. I think I even lost my ability to sing for a while, simply because I wasn't exercising my vocal muscles as I should, and as I used to do when I was young. I guess it's a bit like kids who play a lot of sport when they are at school and then lose the habit as other things like work and families gradually take over their lives.

But then, as we moved into the 1990s, my ambition to sing began to rekindle deep inside me. Once Alexandra was old enough for me to feel happy about leaving her with Mum and the others in the evenings, I started going to singers' open-mic nights some weekends. Just to watch, mind you, because I still felt too self-conscious to think about going back to singing in public. What happens at these nights is that a DJ sets up some acoustic music, there may even be a few instruments around if people want to use them, and people put their names down to perform and are then called up in turn through the evening to take the stage. It's a good place to try stuff out because people are so busy dancing and talking they don't take much notice if you are rubbish, or if you are just ordinary. But if you are good you can really catch the crowd's attention and get them cheering you on.

People love to discover new talent, to feel that they are in on the beginning of something big and special. I believe that explains the success of all the talent shows from *Opportunity Knocks* and *New Faces* all the way through to *Pop Idol*, *Fame Academy* and *The X Factor*. On the one hand, audiences like to see people making fools of themselves, even if it causes them to squirm with embarrassment, because it reassures them that they aren't the only ones who are bad at things and because they like to see people who seem to have false ideas of how good they are being brought down to size. But on the other hand they also like to be blown away by something unexpectedly good. Perhaps that makes them feel, for a few moments at least, as if they too might one day be discovered and bask in sudden glory. The moment when Susan Boyle started to sing 'I Dreamed a Dream' on *Britain's Got Talent* was probably the ultimate feel-good moment that everyone who attends open-mic nights is hoping for, which was why so many millions of people all over the world tuned in to see it again and again on YouTube.

When I met up with my sister Frances's youngest daughter, Dionne, who I hadn't seen for years, I found out she was signed to a major record company. She and her sisters were wonderful singers and I envied them their confidence to stand up in front of audiences. Listening to them talk reminded me of all the dreams I used to nurture of cutting a record, and made me disappointed with myself for not pushing a little bit harder to overcome my shyness and make the most of the opportunities which had come my way but which I had allowed to pass by.

All the time I was in Retro and Impulse, I kept hoping that some Simon Cowell-type figure would hear me singing and be so impressed they would sign me up and sweep me off to stardom without me having to embarrass myself by going around begging to be given a chance, auditioning and risking rejection day in and day out. There are so many hopefuls banging on the doors of the people who are in a position to make or break them it's hardly surprising that anyone with any influence only opens their door to a very select and lucky few. I would still have loved to have been given the opportunity to be a singer but I think a part of me had accepted that it would probably never happen now.

It's so important to keep your dreams alive. If you allow them to be pushed to one side or crushed by other people, you have allowed a little bit of yourself to die. We need hopes and dreams to look forward to, to give us a reason to get up in the morning and struggle through another day, even if they eventually turn out to have been fantasies.

One experience brought it home to me that once you are out there performing you never know who is listening. Ian Levine, the songwriter and producer who has been involved with everyone from the Pet Shop Boys to Erasure, Kim Wilde to Bronski Beat and Bananarama to Take That, got to hear me singing at an open-mic night and contacted me through a friend. I think maybe someone had recorded me and he heard it on the internet first. Anyway I went up to his studio off the M4 and we put together a track called 'Innocent Till Proven Guilty'. Ian wrote the lyrics but the melody line is mine. The track has gone on to one of his compilation albums, which sell millions of copies around the world and at his mansion we shot a video which is now up on YouTube.

Another evening, Dionne took me to a West Indian restaurant that she went to regularly, where she knew there would be a live band playing. Without saying anything to me, she slipped away from the table during the meal and whispered to the band leader that I had a great voice and that he should call me up to the stage. Her face gave nothing away as she came back to sit down and I was feeling very relaxed and happy as I looked forward to my food and enjoyed the music.

Halfway through my jerk chicken, rice and peas, however, I heard an announcement that sent real shivers down my spine and made me flush simultaneously hot and cold, if that is possible.

'Is there a singer called Mel in here tonight?' a voice asked over the public announcement system.

I told myself not to be silly, that there must be another

Mel in the room somewhere. I put in another mouthful of food and looked around to see who they were talking about, only to find everyone pointing me out and cheering wildly. I nearly choked as I tried to chew and swallow and protest at the same time as the spotlight found me and pinned me in its beam.

'Ladies and gentlemen,' the amplified voice went on, 'please welcome Mel up to the stage.'

I was terrified, like a rabbit in the headlights just waiting for the wheels of the oncoming lorry to hit me. It had been so long since I had stood on a stage that it almost felt like I was now a different person, someone who would never dream of doing something like this. I would have run away if I had thought my legs would support me. But I was excited at the same time as scared. Dionne pulled me to my feet and propelled me towards the stage, refusing to listen to my increasingly half-hearted protests. I was in a daze as someone else handed me a live mic. The band began to play the opening bars of 'Loving You' by Minnie Riperton. Minnie was a fabulous artist who tragically died from cancer in 1979 at the age of 31. It's said she died in her husband's arms in the Cedars-Sinai Medical Center in Los Angeles, listening to a recording that Stevie Wonder had made for her.

I closed my eyes to avoid the stare of the audience, took my cue from the music and sang my heart out, remembering how I had felt about David when I first saw him standing astride his bike in Kingston, looking so sharp and beautiful, before the dream had soured between us.

As I sang, I could feel my fear draining away and I could

hear that my voice sounded strong and true through the sound system. When I finished I heard rapturous applause and saw a room full of faces staring at me, smiling, laughing and cheering. The tears welled up in my eyes and rolled down my cheeks but I didn't care. I had given my first performance in years and in that moment had caught the singing bug once more. For too long the failure of my marriage had made me feel like I was a failure too, but the applause told me something different, making me feel that maybe I wasn't such a lost cause after all.

Later that same night, the band leader came over to sit with us for a drink and asked me to join his music crew as one of the session singers, performing on a regular basis. An invitation was all I needed and I jumped at it, accepting instantly, eager to recapture the excitement I had experienced when I had sung in public as a girl. Every Thursday after that, we met and performed for free at the restaurant, always being given a lovely West Indian meal as our reward. I was truly 'singing for my supper'. The audience was always friendly and enjoyed whatever we did. Slowly, my self-confidence grew and I felt my singing muscles flexing and strengthening once more with the exercise.

The session singers' crew performed at a lot of big festivals and events and I was able to sing with them, just like in the old days with the bands. It was just what I needed to get my life back on track, to remind myself that a marriage that hadn't worked out didn't have to mean the end of anything, that it might even allow me to begin again. Maybe music was meant to be my life all along and getting married had just been a wrong turning in the road.

CHAPTER FIFTEEN

THE BREAKTHROUGH SONG

M um's diabetes was growing much worse. She never had to inject herself but she was always taking tablets and having to watch her diet. Over the years, I had grown used to it, almost taking it for granted. When I was younger, I would come running into the house with bags full of sweets, wanting to share them with her, but she always said no. She was good at resisting temptation in that way, much better than me. When we went to Jamaica, the neighbours would make Kool-Aid to combat the fierce heat of the days. It was a drink I had never come across in England, and one of the few things I liked about being out there, but Mum would never take any because it was too highly sugared and her body wasn't making the insulin that we all need to turn sugar into energy.

I didn't really understand why she wasn't allowed these things. When you're small you just accept what grown-ups tell you and only really question the reasons later, when the same experiences start to happen to you. She never gave me any reason to be concerned for her because she lived a perfectly normal life until the moment that her kidneys failed in 1990, which was when all our lives changed dramatically again.

After her kidneys finally failed completely, she went into hospital for a year, but she couldn't be given dialysis. Although the doctors would do what they could to help her cope with the terrible symptoms of the illness, there weren't enough machines for everyone with kidney failure to be allocated one, and so anyone who was over 60 had to be excluded, which meant it was only a matter of time before they would die. The authorities who made the rules had to decide which patients would benefit most from the treatment that would keep them alive and functioning as close to normal as possible, and young people with their lives ahead of them were given priority. Although we could understand the reasoning behind this decision, for us as a family it was heartbreaking to know that there were machines in existence that could save Mum from all her suffering and prolong her life, but that she wasn't considered useful enough to society to be given access to one.

It was obvious when she eventually came home from the hospital that she was going to need to be looked after on a full-time basis and so I gave up my job at M&S. It wasn't going to be possible to look after her at the same time as bringing up three children and working. Although I was very sad to be leaving the company because I had loved my time there, I couldn't help but think that maybe this was my chance to put some more time into developing my singing career. I'm sure everything happens for a reason, even the really bad stuff.

I was still going to as many talent shows as possible, wanting to watch and meet other performers in order to learn how to do things better and perhaps to find someone who would be able to help me move forward with my career. Most nights nothing happened, but one night at a talent show at the Hackney Empire I experienced a breakthrough.

The Empire is a fantastic East End venue, one of the classic old London theatres. It was built in 1901 and Charlie Chaplin and Stan Laurel (who later became one half of Laurel and Hardy) both used to appear there before they headed for Hollywood and became two of the biggest and earliest movie stars in the world.

In its early days, the Empire's biggest star was a local girl called Marie Lloyd, 'The Queen of the Halls', who was famous for songs like 'The Boy I Love Is Up in the Gallery', 'A Little of What You Fancy' and 'Oh, Mr Porter'. I've seen pictures of her and I think she must have been a bit like the Cilla Black of her day, although her material would have been a lot more shocking and near the knuckle. Like many people in those days, Marie was part of a big family and seven of her nine brothers and sisters had theatre acts as well. She was by far the most popular performer of the time, particularly with the working classes, who didn't have much choice of entertainment in that era, and it's said that over a hundred thousand people turned up to pay their respects at her funeral.

After the Second World War, radio stars like Tony

Hancock and performers like Liberace used to appear at the Empire, and when television first discovered pop music they used to film a show called *Oh Boy!* (an early version of *Top Of The Pops*) there, with stars including Cliff Richard and Marty Wilde.

It then became little more than a bingo hall until the 1980s, when it was restored to its former glories with the help of people like Griff Rhys Jones and Alan Sugar (a Hackney lad) and became one of the most important venues for stand-up comedians who were trying to break into the big time.

The show that I had gone to see was for singers and was all about the audience encouraging the acts they liked and booing off the ones they didn't. They were a hard audience to please that night. Nearly all of them were booing everyone off within a few seconds of them coming on, like several hundred would-be Roman emperors voting for the slaughter of gladiators at the Coliseum.

'Well,' the presenter told us as the last one was sent packing, 'you're all dumb because now the show's over. You've sent home all the acts. So, if you want the show to go on, how about some of you stepping forward and seeing if you can do any better? Is there anyone in the audience who can sing? Is there anyone out there who has the nerve to stand up here and face the crowd like all those guys did?'

Maybe it was because I didn't have time to think about it that I found the courage to stick up my hand and shout, 'I will!' Or maybe it was just my destiny that night. Whatever the reason, that's what I did, surprising even myself.

'Aha,' said the presenter, jumping at the chance to get the show going again. 'There's a young lady out there who thinks she can sing!'

The next thing I knew he was down off the stage and coming up through the audience to find me, with microphone and cameras in tow, cables snaking along the floor behind them. They had scented fresh blood and they were pouncing before I had a chance to change my mind and make a run for the exit. There was no going back now. My heart was thumping and I felt like I was going to faint, yet I was ready to sing. He thrust the mic in my face with the cameras peering over his shoulders at me and I felt five hundred faces craning to see who was about to make a fool of themselves for their pleasure now.

As soon as I started to sing, I could tell that it was coming out strong and clear. The crowd fell silent for a few moments and then began to clap and cheer their encouragement. The presenter looked relieved to find that he was going to be able to get the show moving again. He took my hand and led me up on to the stage so everyone could see me properly. There was a lot of encouraging applause, like they were willing me on to be good, wanting to be entertained.

After taking a deep breath, I began to sing 'Memories', from the Streisand and Redford film *The Way We Were*, a song which Gladys Knight recorded too. It's such a pure, moving song with lyrics about beautiful, painful memories that anyone can identify with it. I got all the way through it with no backing music, just my voice ringing round the quiet auditorium and then a roar of applause at the end as the whole audience rose to their feet, delighted by the surprise of finding someone they liked sitting in their midst: one of their own.

Afterwards, while I was still feeling giddy from the rush of adrenalin and the excitement of all the compliments and admiration being poured over me, a guy called Scotty emerged from the crush of bodies around me in the bar and introduced himself, saying he worked as a producer for an indie record label. He wrote down his number and gave it to me. I don't know if I would ever have called him if I hadn't met another friend, who had worked in the warehouse at M&S when I was there and who knew Scotty and said he was OK. So the next day I phoned and arranged to go up to Wood Green and see the company. The meeting went well. They played a lot of the songs they had made and I recognised them from the radio, which was exciting. It seemed like I might finally be going to get my voice committed to vinyl, the dream I had been carrying around with me almost all my life.

'I can put you on a record,' Scotty said, as if reading my mind. 'And I can make it a hit.'

I liked the whole team and went back to the studio a few days later to record a track which I wrote on the spot. I've always been good at improvising like that. Sometimes, when I'm singing a song which I don't know all that well, I just make up my own words as I go along and it always works. It probably took me no more than 15 minutes to write that song, and less than an hour to record it, but it ended up changing my life.

'This is going to be a hit,' everyone in the studio said

when we'd finished, but I didn't dare to believe it, not till it happened.

They released it anonymously on a white-label disc in order to build up a bit of curiosity and hype. The song was called 'Reconsider' and it became the fastest-selling street song of the year despite the fact that the production company had virtually no marketing or advertising expertise, relying almost completely on word-of-mouth recommendations to get the song aired. It started to get played and talked about on radio stations and the DJs were all asking who this anonymous singer was, offering rewards to anyone who had information.

Mum was bedridden by that stage and Dad and I were taking turns to look after her. She had a radio by her bedside and she was constantly flicking between different stations in the hope of hearing my record. By chance I was in the room with her when she finally struck lucky and I watched the glow of pride on her tired old face as she listened, smiling and nodding her approval to me.

Although the company got the record out there on the airwaves, they weren't equipped to help me build any sort of permanent career on the back of its success. But having a hit opened other doors for me, increasing the number of people in the music industry who knew about me and liked what I did, widening my network and giving me more credibility.

I started to receive calls and approaches from people asking me to sing for them, one of which was an invitation to be a backing singer at a giant Freddie Mercury tribute concert being staged at Wembley Stadium on Easter

Monday, 20 April 1992. If I accepted, I would be singing with members of the London Community Gospel Choir behind names like Elton John, David Bowie, George Michael, Liza Minnelli, Lisa Stansfield, Guns N' Roses and Annie Lennox.

Freddie had died the year before and all the proceeds were going to an AIDS charity called the Mercury Phoenix Trust. Brian May and Roger Taylor had announced the event at the Brit Awards and all 72,000 tickets had been sold in four hours, even before any of the acts had even been announced apart from themselves and John Deacon (the fourth member of Queen). I think it took me about five seconds to decide that I wanted to do it but it was a bit longer before it started to dawn on me just what a huge deal it was going to be.

Stadium rock concerts are some of the greatest spectator events of modern times. The bone-shaking beat of the bass lines coming up through your feet, the soaring guitars and voices and the excitement of the crowds made up of tens of thousands of people looking to have a good time all come together amid the lights and the hype to lift everyone's spirits and carry them to a different place for a few hours. If it feels like that to be in the audience, imagine how great it feels to be up on the stage in the middle of the fireworks, the amplifiers and the superstars.

At that moment, as I stood up there on the stage looking out over the heads of more than seventy thousand people, belting out some of the greatest songs in popular music, I knew I was in exactly the right place at the right time. For those few hours, there can't have been a better place on the planet to be standing than in the centre of that stage. The organisers reckoned that over a billion people tuned in to watch us live on television that day, across all the time zones. Everyone loved Freddie, loved the music and loved the other stars who were bringing it to them. What an incredible buzz it is when so much good feeling comes together in one place. When I received a call from a friend in Israel while I was backstage between numbers, telling me that they were watching the concert live and had seen me up on the screen, I knew it was going global for real.

It is the hope of experiencing this sort of high that keeps all of us struggling on in a business which is one of the most competitive, difficult and potentially heartbreaking in the world. Looking back, it doesn't matter how many times you have sung to tiny audiences who were more interested in eating their dinner than listening to you, or how often you have been paid peanuts for giving a performance that in other circumstances might have been worth millions, because those are all integral parts of the apprenticeship you have to serve. Every frustration and disappointment has a purpose; they are all preparing you for the big moments in the spotlight.

The trouble is you never know when the truly great moments are going to arrive, or even if they ever will. But you have to believe until all hope is gone, and I think sometimes the disappointment breaks the hearts of the people who are never lucky enough to get their moments in the sunshine. Maybe that was another reason why so many people identified with Susan Boyle and her performance on *Britain's Got Talent*. She looked like someone whose hopes of ever becoming a star had almost faded out, but then her opportunity came and she was ready to grasp it, even though the intensity of the experience nearly knocked her off balance emotionally afterwards.

Some full-time backing singers are able to make huge amounts of money from their voices, but they can only really do that by touring with the stars all the time, which is impossible if you have a family to take care of. I was asked to tour with a lot of people, such as Depeche Mode, who were big at the time after breaking through at the beginning of the 1980s with the single 'Just Can't Get Enough'. They had been formed in 1980 and went on to be one of the longest-lasting acts of that period, having over 40 hit singles and albums that went to number one on both sides of the Atlantic. Their keyboard player and songwriter Vince Clarke later left to form Yazoo with Alison Moyet and Erasure with Andy Bell.

I loved doing the actual singing and performing, but I didn't love it enough to sacrifice being with my kids during their growing-up years, which is what would have happened if I had gone out on the road. Even if I had wanted to, how could I have done that to them when their father had already walked out on them? Once you have children, I think everything else has to take second place until they are adults and able to take care of themselves.

Just releasing a record was a huge excitement for me. Once a song is recorded and out there, you never know who might be listening to it. 'Reconsider' was heard by Jazzy B, who played it on his show on Kiss FM and tracked me down to ask me to be lead singer of his collective, Soul II Soul, who were making 'Black British Music', a mix of soul, reggae, funk and European music. They had won two Grammys and had big hits with 'Keep on Movin'', which was featured in *Grand Theft Auto: San Andreas* and 'Back to Life', which was used in one of those ads for the Renault Clio with the father and daughter ('Papa' and 'Nicole', if you are old enough to remember).

Born and brought up in north London, Jazzy had always wanted to be a DJ, playing his music at house and street parties, and at the Africa Centre in Covent Garden. He had a studio up the road from where I was living, and I agreed to go there to audition for him. He asked me to join the band and even kept my intro from that audition and released it on his next album, although I had to re-sing the rest of the song. Jazzy liked using different people all the time in order to get different sounds.

It felt like there was a lot happening in my career, like my dreams might finally be coming true, but none of this activity was bringing in money, certainly not enough to support me and the kids. I wanted to stay self-employed so that I could take advantage of every opportunity that came up as well as having time to help look after Mum. Once you have a normal full-time job, it becomes really hard to go to auditions or recordings or gigs: you need flexibility to be able to take advantage of opportunities when they arise. It's probably the main reason why so many people who set out to be performers aren't able to stay in the business, why they eventually have to give up and look for a steadier way to make a living.

In the end, I was actually working much harder than I ever had when I was going in to M&S nine to five every day. At one stage I was doing three different jobs. I was doing picture framing for a friend who worked for some sort of advertising company and would bring me all the materials so that I could work at home. I would also do telephone sales from home and then at night go out cleaning offices in the centre of town, close to UCH, where Mum had worked as a nurse. I hated the cleaning the most, mainly because it involved emptying dirty ashtrays, which was a disgusting, smelly job, like being in another universe compared with my times on stage or in the recording studio. It was exhausting, too, but at least the hours were flexible, and I just had to keep telling myself that it was all a means to an end, a way of surviving until something better turned up.

As part of Soul II Soul, I recorded 'Wish', made a video, appeared on *Top Of The Pops* and travelled with them to perform in places like Spain and Dubai. But, although it was a lucky break, it never felt like a long-term career move. Sure enough, they lost their record deal soon after that and I went back to earning a steady living and being a mum.

I was learning that, even when you get the breaks, they don't always lead on to other things in the way you would hope. And that more often they just melt away to nothing unless you keep on working at them, unless you keep your ambition alive. I had been allowed some tastes of the sweet life and I was grateful for those, but that didn't mean I wasn't still hungry for more. I wasn't ready to settle down in the rocking chair on the porch just yet.

CHAPTER SIXTEEN

THE FUNERAL PLAN

When he first heard that Mum's kidneys had failed, Dad came home with a present for her: a funeral plan which he had paid for in full.

He meant well, not wanting her to be worried about how we would pay for her funeral expenses once she had gone, but it was a shock for me when he came in with the booklet and handed it over to her as though it was the most normal thing in the world. Suddenly it was brought home to me that my mother was not immortal, that it was extremely likely she was going to die quite soon. It was a concept I could barely get my head round and, to be honest, I'm not sure Mum had completely taken all the inevitable implications of kidney failure on board until that moment.

Once her kidneys had stopped functioning, however, the illness progressed with a terrible and visible speed. Even when she was out of bed and sitting in the chair, it was easy to see that her ankles were swollen like an elephant's legs as the fluid and poisons accumulated inside her. I could see how ill she was but I didn't really understand the medical implications of why she was becoming the way she was. Nowadays, I would be going straight to the internet to look up any symptoms that anyone in the family might develop. All I knew then was that I had to give her tablets at the times the doctor said and I had to cook her meals and help her to stay clean. I didn't ask too many questions, I just got on with what had to be done, developing new routines to deal with each new need that arose.

After a while, I managed to get a *Reader's Digest* book on the subject, which helped a bit, but perhaps if I had been able to understand earlier what was going on inside her I could have been of more help to her. Perhaps if she had known more about the way the body works she would have taken better care of herself and would have been able to do more to teach me as a child how to take better care of myself too. But no one was as open or free with medical information and advice in those days. Even in the 1990s, the doctors seemed to be surprised that someone like me knew anything at all when I went in with her to see them and tried to ask questions, tried to understand better what was happening.

'Are you a nurse?' they would ask, not realising that I was just quoting verbatim whatever it was that I had read in the book, my understanding only growing very slowly. They still never seemed keen to explain anything in any detail unless they were pressed for answers, and even then they were often trying to avoid giving a full explanation. I think they had us down as ignorant people, believing they would be wasting their time if they tried to explain things, just wanting us to do as we were told and not ask questions. Or maybe they didn't want to frighten us with too many details of what lay ahead.

Dad was even less clued up than I was about the medical side of what was going on inside Mum, simply concentrating on taking care of her daily needs while getting on with his own life at the same time. The swelling in her feet became terrible to see, and dramatic dark circles under her eyes made it look like she hadn't slept for years. Her hair started to fall out and when she developed gangrene the stench became overwhelming and they had to amputate one of her toes before it spread. It was as if her whole body was giving up on her, rotting away piece by piece.

She developed congestive heart failure and throughout 1992 the problems became worse and worse.

This was a time when George Michael and Elton John were singing 'Don't Let the Sun Go Down on Me' together, and Mary J. Blige was exploding on to the scene with songs like 'You Remind Me' and 'Real Love'.

Time changes so many things and as the years went past David never stopped asking me to take him back, promising me that he had changed his ways, that he had learned his lesson and would never treat me badly again. I wanted to believe him so much, even though part of me knew all along that he was fooling himself if he believed that he was capable of being a good husband and father. But another part of me wanted to think that it was possible for someone to change for the better. Bringing up three children on your own is hard, and what woman wouldn't prefer to have the father of her children around if she has a choice, especially if she loves the man and believes that he loves her too? On top of that, I was now having to look after Mum, instead of her being able to offer me support, which meant I was struggling all the more to cope with the demands every new day brought.

Despite always having a house full of people and animals, there were times when I felt the loneliness of not having a partner and in a weak moment I agreed to take David back and give him another chance. For a very short time, it actually seemed as if I had made the right choice and he had mended some of his ways, although he still wasn't any help around the house. In some ways, it was like having yet another person to look after, but at the same time it was good not to feel so alone.

A few months later, I discovered that I was pregnant again, for the fourth time, and everything in our lives seemed to be even more stressful as Mum's condition continued to deteriorate fast and she was taken into hospital with no predictions from the doctors as to whether she would come out again.

It seemed inevitable that she was going to die sooner rather than later, but the doctors couldn't give us any idea how long she was likely to last. I had booked us all a week's break in a caravan in Cornwall in August and as the date of the holiday drew nearer Mum's condition seemed to be stabilising a little. I felt terribly torn because I could see that she couldn't be taken away on holiday, not even for a week, and I didn't want to leave her in hospital and travel to the other end of the country. But at the same time I could see that David and the kids all needed a break, and I knew that I certainly did. The caravan was paid for in advance, and when I pressed the doctors they told me they thought Mum had a few months left in her. Dad said we should go for a few days and he would stay with Mum.

Even after we had made the decision, it still didn't feel quite right to me as we drove down to the far south-west of the country, miles away from where I knew she was lying in her bed, struggling to stay alive. Each evening, I would ring the ward for an update on how she was doing and each time the answer was the same – 'no change' – and we went back to trying to enjoy our holiday for another 24 hours, if only for the sake of the kids. Then one evening the nurse who answered the phone put my sister on the line.

'I think you need to come home,' she said. 'Mum's developed pneumonia and they don't know how long she will last.'

It was like I was inside my own worst nightmare. All I wanted was to be sitting beside her bed, holding her hand, instead of which I was several hundred miles away, unable to comfort her or to tell her how much I loved her. I was terrified I wouldn't get back in time to say goodbye.

We had made some friends at the holiday camp who helped us to pack quickly, hurling everything into the back of the car as we tried to settle the children for an unexpected journey without alarming them. We were on the road within an hour, heading back towards London as the sky grew dark above us and the children went off to sleep in the back seat. David was doing all the driving because of my condition and halfway there we had to stop at a motorway service station so that he could rest for a few hours. The time was ticking away and there was nothing I could do about it. I could hardly force him to pull back on to the road if he was tired when we had the kids in the car with us.

We eventually ran into the hospital at 7.30 in the morning and I galloped straight up to the Intensive Care Unit as fast as my size would allow.

'I've come to see Ivy Ewen,' I told the nurse, panting for breath.

She gently led me into a side room where my sister and Dad were sitting, looking like their world had ended, and I knew she had gone. I felt the terrible scream rising up inside me even before it came out. I was so horrified to find that I hadn't been there for her at the end I could hardly bear the pain. It was like I was in shock. She had died only a quarter of an hour before, just as we were struggling to find a parking space outside the hospital. After a few minutes, they all managed to calm me down enough for me to be able to go behind the screens to her bedside to see her. She looked very peaceful but the sight of her body and my inability to say goodbye to her were too much to bear. I couldn't stop sobbing.

Eventually, I was drained and the nurses led me out from behind the screens and back to the side room.

'I'm going to work,' Dad announced, looking at his watch and getting to his feet as I came in.

'What?' I wasn't sure I'd heard him right. How could he

just continue on as if nothing had happened, as if everything in our lives was normal?

'That is how I am going to deal with this,' he said firmly. 'I have to just keep going, give myself something to think about.'

When I stopped to think about it, I could understand his thinking. What was the point of sitting in the hospital feeling sorry for ourselves? Life had to go on, although at that moment I couldn't imagine how.

'OK,' I said. 'We'll all go.'

As David drove us home, I was still in a state of shock. Even the following day, I was unable to take in what had happened and what it meant to me. In my head, I knew that life had to continue, but it didn't feel like it was possible. We went out to the local Kentucky Fried Chicken because the children were hungry, but I couldn't bring myself to eat anything knowing that Mum was lying in the mortuary and would never be able to eat again. Once the kids were finished, we walked round the market and I was in a daze. We bumped into a man I hadn't seen for years, not since we were both 16. He was the son of the owner of a club that I used to go to many years before. I had forgotten how good-looking and charming he was. A couple of months later, I heard that he had been killed in a car crash and it was yet more confirmation of how fragile life was and how easily it could be lost.

Mum was partly Church of England and partly Church of Christ, which was the gospel church she and Dad had become so involved with. We had a service with lots of people coming up to the microphone to speak about her or to sing songs. West Indian funerals aren't solemn occasions at all and after the burial you go on to a major party which is often held in a hall or some other communal space and is packed with performers, dancers, sound systems and musicians. Because I was heavily pregnant and deeply distraught about the whole thing, I wasn't on top form for taking care of the organisation, not having had to do anything like it before, and Dad was never good at that sort of thing. The funeral itself was all paid for, so we buried her with her mother and then we just went back to her house for some food and music.

All my emotions seemed to be in a heightened state as a result of the pregnancy and the bereavement, not to mention all the underlying stresses of trying to rebuild my marriage into something worthwhile, and coping with Mum's illness for so long. When the hearse pulled up at the house on the day of the funeral, the thought of Mum lying in the coffin inside pushed me over the edge again, sending me wailing and sobbing into the arms of those around me. On the surface, it might have looked like I was coping with everything life was throwing at me, but underneath I must have been in turmoil.

The party afterwards was a nice, affectionate send-off for her from all the people who loved her, but looking back now I can see she deserved a bigger event and I regret that. She was a great mum and a great grandmother and now I was going to have to manage without her.

CHAPTER SEVENTEEN

GRANDDAD TO THE RESCUE

Aaron was born five weeks early and weighed 8lb 5oz, which made him the smallest of all my babies. He was our fourth child and second son, and by the time he arrived in the family, five weeks after we buried Mum with her mother in Enfield Cemetery, I had discovered that David was betraying me again. In fact, I doubt if he ever stopped betraying me, whatever he might have been saying to my face.

He may have made a bit of an effort to protect me from the truth when we first got back together but eventually he didn't even bother to be that subtle about trying to hide it from me. I walked into the kitchen at home one day and found him on the mobile phone, flirting and laughing like it was the most natural thing in the world. Mobiles were still pretty primitive in those days and I could clearly hear the woman's voice at the other end. He made some half-hearted attempts to deny it when I accused him (shades of Shaggy's 'It Wasn't Me' song again), but it was obvious he was lying and his arrogant, dismissive attitude, coming so soon after all the promises he had made about changing his ways, threw me into a violent rage.

David had a red Vauxhall Cavalier that he had bought from a showroom opposite his previous mistress's flat. Officially, it was my car as well but I had never had a chance to drive it because he was always using it to visit his various girlfriends, or whatever it was he got up to when he was out of my sight. Boiling with fury at being let down and hurt yet again, and possibly angry with myself for being so stupid as to allow him to talk me into taking him back, I stormed out of the house, grabbed some bricks off a nearby builder's pile and started bombarding his precious car. I was smashing the windscreen, the lights, the paintwork, oblivious to the curious stares from the neighbours as they peered nervously out from behind their curtains to see what all the noise was about. I suppose it was stupid of me to destroy a car that was half mine, but I didn't care, and I wanted him to have to walk and catch buses everywhere for a change, like the rest of us.

Any woman who has been in love will understand how I had been led into making the mistake of taking him back and having another child with him, but I want them to know that it is always possible for any woman faced with that choice to stand on her own and retain her dignity if she is determined enough. Just because you are in love with a man doesn't mean you have to end up being a doormat to him. You can always decide you have had enough and call a stop to everything. I had been wrong to give him another chance and I was never going to make the same mistake again.

At that moment, I accepted all the things that I had probably known deep down already. I knew he was never going to change and that I would never be able to trust him again no matter what he promised or how hard he pleaded for forgiveness. That day I threw him out of the house once and for all, vowing to bring up the four children on my own, just as I had been doing with the first three before he came back. It was soon obvious that that was exactly what I was going to have to do too, because David never contributed a single penny to the upbringing of his children after that, even when he started a successful restaurant business and began to become quite rich. If I had known how hard things were going to become in the next few years, I might not have had the courage to throw him out when I did, but I've never regretted doing it.

Aaron was four years younger than Alex. So I now had four children under eight years of age with no husband and no mother to help me look after them, and my health was growing worse, although I didn't like to admit that to anyone, not even to myself.

Dad came to my rescue and helped me with the kids. I don't know how we would have coped without him there during those difficult years. He never complained for a second about all the responsibilities that I had to heap on him, always giving the impression that he loved every moment of being with us, even though he was still doing shifts at the dry cleaner's and must have felt as exhausted as I did some days. As he was now widowed, I guess it gave him something to do and made him feel like he was still useful in the world. I suspect a lot of elderly people end up feeling they are surplus to requirements, just a burden on the younger members of the family, but with Dad it was completely the opposite.

Although he kept his own flat on, he was with us most of the time. I believe he felt that in a way David and Aaron were the sons he never had and he did everything that a father should do for them and for the girls. I had felt sad for some time to think that his surname would end with him because he had only had daughters, both of whom had taken the names of their husbands. Although I didn't think of it in time to include 'Ewen' among Sheniece's names, I had made sure all the others had it as one of their middle names, to ensure that it would live on after he had gone. I hope when they have children they will do the same, to honour the memory of everything he did for them when they were young.

Every day he would drive to work in the morning and then pick them up from school in the little orangey-red BMW we had bought from the small ads for his job. The car was nearly 30 years old and had cost us about £800 but we all loved it and thought it was the flashest thing ever. Dad and I went halves on buying and running it as he only really needed it because he had to get to work from my house and then back to the school, so it didn't seem fair that he should have to pay for it all himself. Before that, he had been able to walk to work from his house and had virtually no overheads.

When the kids came running out of school, Dad would

be waiting outside for them. He would take them to the play park, sitting patiently and uncomplainingly on a bench, reading and re-reading his *Daily Mirror*, sipping contentedly on a can of Special Brew, watching over them for as long as they wanted to stay, only bringing them home once they started to get hungry. Every day he would cook dinner for them, which always meant his favourite dish of spicy Jamaican chicken and rice, which he put in the oven before he went to collect them so it would be ready when they eventually got home. The kids grew to dread it.

'Oh, Granddad,' they would sigh as they came into the house to be greeted by the delicious but all-too-familiar aromas. 'You've done Jamaican chicken and rice again.'

'Yes,' he would reply airily, choosing to ignore the despondent looks on their faces. 'And bloody good chicken and rice it is too.'

If it hadn't been for Dad during those years, I wouldn't have been able to keep working at whatever jobs I could find. Knowing he was always there to back me up gave me a fantastic strength and I don't know how I would have managed through those years without him. In 1995, he even paid for me to have a week's holiday with Pam, a friend of mine from my M&S days. We went to the island of Kos in Greece and that was where I first met Angela. I was sitting outside a popular café, reading a Jackie Collins novel and relaxing, when I noticed a beautiful six-foot brunette looking down at me.

'Excuse me,' she said in an Australian accent, 'do you know of any place where they play live music on this island?'

'As a matter of fact, I do,' I replied. 'There's a band from London who play in this place in the evenings and they're really good. Come along this evening. They get members of the audience up on stage to sing with them. I was up with them last night.'

She sat down to talk and I discovered that, although she was from Adelaide, her family was actually Greek. She was travelling alone, tracing her Greek roots, looking up relatives and exploring her parents' culture.

That evening she joined Pam and me for dinner. We went down to the beach and on to Bar Street, which was where all the music and food happened, and met up with two other girls from Australia, Mavi and Denise, and Bibi from Holland. During the course of the evening, I discovered that not only was Angela beautiful, she was funny and outgoing as well, and she shared my passion for singing. By the end of the night, we had become firm friends.

Back in London, a couple of months later, all four of the girls from that night out, including Angela, descended on my little house for a reunion, filling every inch of the place with laughter at shared memories of the holiday, and Angela pretty much moved in from then on, becoming the kids' beloved 'Aunty Ange'.

She became so much a part of the family that Aaron, who was still only three, actually thought he had a Greek mum for a while. Ange would help me round the house during the day, sharing the job of collecting the kids from school and cooking meals with Dad, and we would write songs and go to open-mic nights together at the weekends.

'This woman can't be your aunty,' one of Sheniece's friends told her one day.

'Why not?' Sheniece wanted to know.

'Because she's white and you're black.'

'She's my mum's "soul sister",' Sheniece retorted, 'so that makes her my aunty.'

Eventually, Angela decided that her holiday was over and she got a job and moved out, to a flat a few doors away from us, which meant the kids then had two homes to run back and forth between.

It wasn't until many years later, when Angela had gone back to Australia and I went down to visit her, that I discovered she came from a very wealthy family. I admired her all the more for the fact that she had never mentioned it, wanting to be sure that people liked her for herself and not for her money, and I also admired her for the fact that she always worked to support herself and never sponged off her parents.

By the end of the 1990s, I was beginning to feel really ill. I would get sudden cramps all over my body, and pins and needles for no reason. My vision was quite often blurred and I noticed that my urine was strange and bubbly. I didn't like to talk to the family about any of it because I knew they would worry and they would tell me to go and see a doctor. In my heart, I think I knew what a doctor would say and it was something I didn't want to hear. I told myself I didn't want them making a fuss, but perhaps I was afraid to put into words the things that I was beginning to think.

Whenever I had a moment to myself, I would look up

all my symptoms on the internet and everything seemed to lead back to kidney disease. I think I kept on searching in the hope that something else would appear, something which would offer an alternative and more benign answer, but it never did. Those two words made my stomach lurch with a particular sense of dread, reminding me of everything I had seen Mum go through during her final years. It seemed like I was reading my own death sentence. I would end up staring at the screen in a daze, not knowing what to do or say, quickly flicking to something else if someone came into the room. I didn't want to talk about it, or even think about it, I just wanted to wait to see what happened with as little fuss and discomfort as possible, trusting to God to do the right thing for me. It was like I had no more energy left for fighting and I felt very alone.

Things grew steadily worse and some days I was too exhausted to even drag myself out of bed, but other days it wasn't so bad and I was able to forget about the fact that I was ill for a few hours and continue to enjoy large parts of my life. On the surface I kidded myself that the illness, whatever it was, would pass, that I was just overtired and run down – but in the small hours, when I was lying awake in bed staring at the ceiling, I knew it was more than that. Having seen the terrible things that happened to Mum, I was frightened to go to the doctors and have it finally confirmed that I was going to have to endure the same thing. I vividly remembered Dad coming home with that funeral plan for Mum. I didn't want to be forced to accept that my life too might now be nearing its end and that the children might be left motherless as well as fatherless while they were still so small. I dived deep into denial.

I half wanted to be left alone to die quietly, in my own way, like a wounded animal crawling into a hedge and waiting for the inevitable to happen. Slowly, slowly, the years went by and the children began to grow up and become more independent.

CHAPTER EIGHTEEN

THE SHOW MUST GO ON

Despite the gradually encroaching illness, however, there were still good times and I could still find a lot of solace in music, both from listening to it and singing. Having growing kids around meant that in our home there was always someone playing something or singing. They were introducing me to a new generation of artists, just as I was introducing them to the greats from the past, the ones whose songs had formed the soundtrack to my own youth.

The whole music scene had changed so much from the days when I had been dependent on a few favourite radio shows, on buying imported vinyl and on recording my own voice on to cassettes. This generation had endless supplies of whatever music they wanted to listen to, from CDs, downloads, iPods, clubs, DJs, dedicated television channels. It has been a wonderful time to be alive if you enjoy music, and I've made the most of it.

When they were little, my four kids even formed a

group. Each of them had an alter ego: Sheniece was 'Jody', David was 'Deejay', Alex was 'Sindy' and Aaron was 'Rocky', and these initials formed the group's name, JDSR. They would make up songs and then record themselves on video. When he was tiny, Aaron was always being left out but by the time he was five he had talked them into letting him be part of the group. Every Sunday we went round to my sister's for dinner and after the meal the chairs would be moved back and JDSR would sing us their 'latest single'.

But as they grew up I realised that neither Sheniece nor David shared my passion for singing. It was a different story with Alexandra. From quite early on, she was clearly a chip off the old block and she was already showing signs of being a little star by the time she was nine. She was constantly putting on shows around the house, recruiting the other kids to be her backing singers, filming their performances with a video camera and then showing us all the results on the television, always hungry for encouragement and praise. It was a long way from the furtive way in which I started, just hoping someone would find out about what I could do and like what they heard. From the start, she seemed to understand how show business worked. I guess it was just the difference between the generations and her antics were the modern equivalent to my early experiments with my radio station in the upstairs window and my cassette machine. Watching the joyful gleam in her eyes when she was performing reminded me of the intensity of the longing that I had felt when I first saw Lena Zavaroni on television and wanted to be in her shoes. I could tell Alex had the same longings, but the difference was she seemed to understand them and knew what she was going to have to do in order to satisfy them.

Even though her voice was still developing, it was already obvious she had a real talent and I encouraged her in every way I could, wanting her to be offered as many opportunities as possible and anxious in case she let them slip through her fingers as I had when I was her age. But at the same time I wanted her to stay in mainstream education. I didn't want to push her into the parallel show-business universe of stage schools like Italia Conti, Sylvia Young or the Brit School, with all the fierce competition and pressure that would inevitably bring. There is no doubt that places like that give young performers a flying start, but there would be plenty of time, I reasoned, for Alex to learn about the business later. To start with, I just wanted to concentrate on developing her singing voice and letting her grow up as a normal kid in every other way.

I tried to guide her away from listening all the time to the acts that were popular with her generation, like the Spice Girls and the boy bands like Louis Walsh's Boyzone and Westlife, and I worked hard to coax her into listening to really good singers like Aretha, Mariah and Whitney, who were doing the sort of material that I knew her voice would eventually be good at.

But it was hard to escape the influence of the Spice Girls if you had children at that time, particularly girls. The band had their first big hit, 'Wannabe', in 1996, when Alex was eight, pretty much the same age as I was when I first fell under the spell of Lena Zavaroni. The impact they had on that generation of girls was incredible. They made everything look possible, five ordinary-seeming girls who became a global phenomenon overnight, selling 23 million copies of their first album. Whereas I'd had role models like the Supremes and Aretha Franklin who already seemed to belong to a distant, glossy world of megastardom and megawealth when I came across them, it was still possible to see exactly where these girls had started out from and what their lives had been like before they got their lucky break. It was easy for a little girl like Alex to identify with them and I didn't want to discourage that positive element, but I did want to make sure that she understood it was possible to sing better than they did. She was very responsive and respectful of anything I suggested, eager to learn and to improve. I wished I'd had the same level of confidence when I was her age.

The whole culture of television talent shows and the music business has changed so much in the past 20 or so years. When a young girl with a good voice talks about being a star and becoming famous, people are less inclined to be discouraging and to put her down than they might have been in the past. There have been too many examples of kids who have been discovered on shows and have become genuine stars, people like Myleene Klass, who started out as part of Hear'Say in *Popstars* in 2001, Girls Aloud, who won *Popstars: The Rivals* in 2002, Will Young who won *Pop Idol* in the same year, Lemar, a Tottenham lad who came third in *Fame Academy* in 2002, and Leona Lewis from the 2006 *X Factor*.

Even the ones who had different levels of success like

Chico and Andy Abrahams – the London bus driver and refuse collector who was in the first *X Factor* that Alex was to enter and who went on to represent Britain in the *Eurovision Song Contest* in 2008 – have managed to build good careers out of appearing on the show and being seen by millions. Even if it all ends for them tomorrow, they have still had fantastic experiences that might otherwise never have come their way.

The hardest thing for any new performer is to get the exposure that is needed to build a fan base and to alert people to what they are capable of, and there have never been so many opportunities for them to do that as there are today. That doesn't mean that it isn't still tough, because the competition is more intense than ever and there are so many talented people out there, each getting their chance in the spotlight. But at least it is possible to see where to start, which was much harder when the music industry and show business were completely different worlds, miles from any ordinary person's experience.

There are always going to be painful knockbacks, because that is what the business is all about (like much of life really). But the vital thing is for young performers to be given enough hope to keep them working towards their goals, to keep them practising and improving their skills, and holding on to their precious dream.

I would take Alex to 'singers' nights' in places like Covent Garden, which were like the open-mic nights I went to myself. Groups of musicians would arrange to meet at a venue, advertising to the public and inviting people on to the stage to have a go. They would make their money from selling drinks over the bar. Even the bad people would be applauded and encouraged, so it was always a positive experience. And this helped kids like Alex to gain a feel for working in front of audiences without the risk of being humiliated in the way they might be later when they came up against industry professionals like Simon Cowell, people who knew exactly what they were looking for and were impatient with anyone who they thought was wasting their time.

'Never be embarrassed by your voice,' I would tell her, knowing from experience how important it was not to be shy about performing if you want to get on. 'It doesn't matter if you make mistakes as long as you try your best. If things go wrong, it will teach you what you need to do to get it right next time. People will only know how good you are if they get to hear you.'

I would encourage Alex to sing at every possible opportunity. If someone asked to hear her in the middle of the street or in a crowded supermarket, I would push her to do it, to help her overcome all her self-consciousness and any fears of failure that might one day hold her back.

'You never know who's listening,' I would say.

To be honest, she never needed telling twice. She was a natural performer and was already starting to behave like a little professional. It lifted my heart to see how much she enjoyed it because I knew how much joy singing had given me over the years.

Each week I always used to buy the show-business trade paper, *The Stage*, just to see who was holding auditions and who was planning shows and productions. Even though a bit of me would have liked to, I seldom answered any of the ads for myself, partly because I didn't have time with a family to look after, partly because I couldn't rely on feeling well enough and partly because of the cost of travelling to wherever the audition was being held. Big auditions often attract hundreds of applicants, so the odds on being picked out are always small, while the expenses involved in getting there are always the same. It's really hard for young performers to find the money they need just to get seen and heard, which is why so many of them end up having to wait on tables and flip burgers in order to earn enough to keep chasing their dreams.

Although I wasn't looking for myself, I started to see talent competitions that I thought Alex might both enjoy and actually stand a chance of winning. When I suggested it to her she responded enthusiastically to the idea. It is madness for any parent to try to get their kids to do this kind of thing against their will. The child has to want it more than anything else if they are going to have any chance of getting anywhere, which is why the talent shows are now so full of tears and monologues from the contestants on how important winning is for them, how performing has always been their dream and how they absolutely 'have to win'.

People have come to expect this from all talent-show contestants, even on things like the cookery competitions. Audiences want to believe that the people they are watching have a burning ambition because that heightens the drama involved in both the winning and the losing. They have to believe that the outcome matters, otherwise there is no tension or suspense. They want to see the hearts of the brave losers being broken and the dreams of the talented winners coming true. A talent contest is like a drama in many ways. As a result, having the passion and hunger for success is almost as important for a contestant as having the talent in the first place – almost, but not quite, of course.

The world is full of people with fabulous voices who would never dream of pushing themselves forward and wouldn't want to go through everything that professional entertainers have to endure on their way to the top, but there aren't many truly talentless people who manage to sustain long careers, whatever the critics and cynical members of the public might think to the contrary.

In the first couple of auditions that I took her to, Alex didn't get through to the next rounds but I wasn't discouraged, believing it was good practice for her to go through the audition process and see what the competition was like. Also, you never know who will see you at those things and decide you might be good for something else. Everything in show business is about networking and timing. As well as all the hard work, you also need an element of luck, which often means no more than being in the right place at the right time. If the right person sees you at a moment when they are keeping an eye out for someone with your abilities or your look, you never know what will come from it. I knew that from my own experiences. If I hadn't gone to the talent show at the Hackney Empire that night in 1990, and hadn't put my hand up when the presenter was asking for volunteers, I would never have met the guys at the record label, would never have had a hit record and would never have got to stand on the stage at Wembley, behind some of the biggest stars in the world. Who could have known when I was getting myself ready to go out that evening that I was about to set that chain of events into motion?

The first audition where Alex got through to appearing on the actual show was a BBC competition called *Star for a Night*. The show was being fronted by Jane MacDonald, a singer who had got her own big break from appearing on a reality series called *The Cruise* and is now most famous for appearing on daytime television in *Loose Women*. Alex was 12 and became best friends with Joss Stone, who eventually won the show, after they met at that audition. Alex got into the final, appearing before 20 million people, and even though she didn't win I felt very encouraged that she had managed to get so far while she was still so young. It seemed like a very promising start to her career.

The moment I saw Joss, who is just over a year older than Alex, walk into the audition room I was sure she would be the winner, even before I had heard her amazing voice performing Aretha's 'You Make Me Feel Like a Natural Woman' and Whitney's 'It's Not Right But It's Okay'. She just looked so beautiful, with her English-rose looks and long blonde hair stretching down below her bottom.

Her career took off immediately after she won the show and her debut album, *The Soul Sessions*, went multi-platinum. Her second album, *Mind Body and Soul*, debuted at number one in the UK, breaking Avril

Lavigne's record for being the youngest female performer ever to achieve this feat. Joss has now sold more than ten million albums, won two BRIT awards at the age of 17 for being Best British Female Solo Artist and Best Urban Artist, and one Grammy. She just keeps on getting better. In 2006, she appeared as the youngest woman in the *Sunday Times* rich list, with a fortune estimated at £6 million. Her success story is an inspiration to all talented young people who are struggling to get their feet on the bottom rungs of the ladder.

People sometimes think that the atmosphere behind the scenes at the talent shows must be horribly competitive and bitchy, but actually it is completely the opposite and we often become close friends with the other competitors and their families after going through such an intense experience together. We always keep an open house for anyone who needs somewhere to sleep and when one of the boys from JLS (the brilliant group who lost in the final to Alexandra) had nowhere to go one Christmas he spent the holiday sleeping on our couch, although I made sure he went home for a bit of Christmas Day in order to see his mum. I keep in contact with a lot of the other mums, texting news back and forth about how the kids are all getting on. It's a nice community of people which has built up through the shared experiences of the talent-show circuit.

I guess the families of the contestants are bound to get on well because we all have so much in common and all want the same things for our kids, but we became particularly close to Joss Stone's family, who were apple farmers from Devon and very down-to-earth people. They would invite Alex to go with Joss on tour to places like America. It was a fantastic opportunity for Alex to see at first hand what the pressures would be like if she kept on the same path herself and it seemed to make her all the more determined to enjoy a similar level of success herself. She was proving to be incredibly strong and focused, which was lucky because my own strength seemed to be ebbing away with frightening speed as the illness took a tighter and tighter grip on my body.

CHAPTER NINETEEN

THE X FACTOR

Just because I was putting so much energy into Alex's future didn't mean that I had given up on my own singing career. I no longer expected to become a big star, and anyway I wouldn't have had the energy for it any more, but I still wanted to be able to perform in front of audiences as often as possible.

I was on a Virgin Atlantic flight when I came across a leaflet about a competition they were doing called Stars in the Sky. It was like their own in-flight talent competition, with heats and finals being held at Richard Branson's house in the country. The prize was a flight to South Africa in first class. I had always fancied the idea of travelling first class on Virgin (I had once been able to travel business class, which was a wonderful experience, so I could imagine what first class must be like). I didn't care what the destination was, so long as I got to be in the best bit of the plane and was able to enjoy all the pampering for a few hours. So I entered and got called to an audition at the house.

The idea was that you had to 'be' a star. It was a bit like *Stars In Their Eyes*, the television series that Matthew Kelly presented where contestants performed as their favourite stars. So I went as a 'fat Whitney Houston', singing 'I Will Always Love You', the incredibly moving Dolly Parton ballad that Whitney has so much made her own after performing it in *The Bodyguard*.

The whole day was like being in heaven, with all the cocktails and food that we could possibly want served up on the lawns. There were about a dozen people competing and I took all the kids with me for a day out. They were given activities and bouncy castles and the whole bit to keep them occupied. It was like being in a private theme park for the afternoon. The only problem was that it was the middle of July, the air was full of pollen and hay fever was affecting my voice. Despite the fact that I knew I wasn't sounding at my absolute best, I could still see, when I started to sing, that everyone in the audience was surprised. It fell completely silent all round the performing area, which was nerve-racking for a few moments as I wasn't sure if it was because they were impressed or horrified by what they were hearing. I could see the famous high note of the song approaching and had no idea if my voice was going to be able to make it through the hay fever. I offered up a silent prayer as I sang and He must have been listening because I got through it to the end and received rapturous applause.

I was put through to the final and when we came back to the house for it they had erected a massive stage, the sort of thing rock groups use in stadiums, and Sir Richard himself was there as well. I didn't win that day, but I did get to talk to him afterwards.

'You used to be my boss,' I said, 'when I sang for Soul II Soul.'

'Oh, yes,' he beamed, 'I remember the videos.'

'You could do me the biggest favour,' I went on, grabbing the opportunity with both hands. 'When we've finished here today, may I send you a demo tape of my daughter, Alexandra? I want it to come straight to you so you can pass it to the right person. She's really good, a star of the future. I'll mark it from "The Fat Whitney in Stars in the Sky", so you'll recognise it.'

'Sure,' he said giving me his card. Nothing ever seems to be a problem for that man.

I sent the CD off the next day and he wrote back immediately to say he had received it and had passed it to the right people in his organisation. A few weeks later, they came back asking if they could hear more. I would have loved to have sent a selection of tracks to show what Alex was capable of but we didn't have the money to record any more at that stage. I still felt encouraged by the reaction, believing that when the time was right it was all going to happen for her. It's amazing how much easier it is to be bold when you are pushing your children's careers rather than your own. I doubt if I would ever have found the courage to talk to someone like Sir Richard about my own career but somehow it seemed like the most natural thing in the world to be doing for Alex. Maybe it was because I had such complete faith in her talent and in her ability to carry off the whole stardom thing. I also felt that I knew enough about singing and the music industry to be able to talk with some authority about her, without sounding like every ambitious but deluded stage mother in history. (Anyone who has ever seen the musical *Gypsy* will know what I mean.)

In 2005, when she was 17, Alex auditioned for the third series of *The X Factor*, and sailed through the early stages, before being selected for the final seven in her category (which meant she was already in the top 30 out of all those thousands of auditionees – an achievement to be proud of), before being sent home from Boot Camp by Louis Walsh before the live shows started because he didn't think the audience was yet 'getting to see the real Alex'.

Although I was just as disappointed as Alex was that it was all over for her, I didn't think it was the end of the road at all. She had appeared in front of millions of people looking great, and she had shown that she could sing. I was confident that with a few more years' experience and practice her voice was going to be truly phenomenal and I already knew that she had the courage and tenacity necessary to keep on trying, despite any setbacks she might encounter. She had already been around long enough to know that if you get knocked down you have to climb straight back up and try again.

That third series was won by Shayne Ward, who was four years older than Alex and had gone through a similar stage of disappointment to the one she was now experiencing when he was knocked out of *Popstars: The Rivals* three years earlier, having reached the final 30 in the series that Girls Aloud went on to win.

Shayne had a huge-selling Christmas single with 'It's My Goal' after winning the contest, and has gone on to sell a load of records, particularly in Japan, where he is an enormous star. If he had been able to come back after his initial disappointment, I was sure Alex would be able to do the same in time. But the following year was too soon for her to apply to *The X Factor* again, which was probably just as well as Leona Lewis was fantastic and became the first female winner. Even if Alex had got to the final, Leona might have eclipsed her, being three years older and having many years of singing and theatre training behind her from the Sylvia Young, Italia Conti and BRIT stage schools, all of which are famous for producing successful performers. (The BRIT School is particularly famous at the moment, having produced Amy Winehouse, Kate Nash, Katie Melua, Imogen Heap, Adele, Noisettes and dozens more.)

I found it encouraging that the public liked Leona's voice. She was even from the same part of London as us; having been born in Islington, she was now living in Hackney.

I'm not sure that Alex would have won if she had entered the following year either, because of the similarities between her and Leona. Would the public have wanted to vote for two big-voiced girl singers in a row? I'm not sure. That year was won by Leon Jackson, who is a few months younger than Alex.

In 2008, however, we were ready to return to the auditions and try again.

CHAPTER TWENTY

KIDNEY FAILURE

Ignoring an illness, of course, is never going to make it go away. Every hour of every day, the disease was ticking away inside me, growing more urgent and more deadly as my kidneys grew less and less effective.

Poisons were spreading around my system and evidence of the damage they were doing was starting to push through to the surface for all to see. Sores, for instance, were breaking out on my feet for no reason. As I looked at them, I remembered the state that Mum's legs used to get into and I knew in my heart that something similar was now happening inside me, that my internal system was starting to collapse. But still I chose not to speak about it to anyone, scared by the prospect of what I might find out if I started to ask questions, not wanting to worry anyone, not wanting to make a fuss, just wanting it all to go away so that I could get on with the good stuff in life.

'Mum, your feet look really bad,' Alexandra said to me

one day in the autumn of 2007. 'You really need to go to see the doctor.'

I tried to skirt round the subject but she wasn't having any of it. It's a strange feeling when your children suddenly start to act like the responsible ones in the relationship. She made the appointment with the doctor on my behalf and made it clear I had no choice but to go. It was like she was the mother and I was the child trying to get out of doing the sensible thing. I remember how shocked I had been at the sight of my mother's ankles when they swelled up and I felt bad that my children might have to go through the same experiences with me. Even when you are technically an adult, it's always a frightening moment when you realise that your parents are not invincible, that they are as mortal as everyone else and that one day they will die and leave you to fend for yourself. I kept the appointment as instructed. The doctor took a blood test and looked grim as he told me the results.

'Your kidneys are diseased,' he said, putting into words what in my heart I already knew.

I couldn't hide from the truth any longer now that other people were involved. It was out in the open and I was going to have to face the scary facts. I took a deep breath and started to ask questions for the first time. I could no longer remain in denial, hiding my head in the sand – not if I wanted to live to see my children successfully launched into their adult lives. I was going to have to accept whatever help might be available.

Apparently, kidney disease goes in five stages, the fifth being actual kidney failure, which is what I have now. At that moment, the doctor told me, I was still at stage four.

'Your kidneys could fail at any moment,' he said, 'or they might keep going for a few more years. It's impossible to predict.'

I chose to listen to the second part of that prognosis and to continue ignoring the possibility that I might soon find myself in the same state as Mum. I wanted to stay optimistic and to pretend that the worst would never happen for as long as possible. Some days I would feel very sick, weary and racked with pain, but I would tell myself I was just having a bad day. It felt like I was being weighed down by something enormous and all I would want to do was sleep. Other days I would feel fine and I would put all thoughts of illness out of my mind, determined to enjoy the moment for as long as it lasted.

One Sunday in July 2008, when Alex was back at home waiting to go to *The X Factor*'s Boot Camp, which wasn't due to start until the beginning of September, she came into the bedroom and found me unable to even haul myself out of bed. The children had all been getting on with their day downstairs as normal, assuming I was just having a lie-in because it was the weekend, but by this time it was late evening and it seemed there was something else happening inside my body beyond mere lethargy. It was such an important time for Alex as she prepared herself for the challenges ahead that I didn't want to make a fuss and cause her any extra worry, but at that moment it was beyond my ability to do anything. I felt too tired to even put up a fight against the illness any more. I was ready to give up, but Alex wasn't having any of that. She was being very businesslike about the whole thing.

'You don't look right, Mum,' she said. 'You're a black woman but you look pale. I'm calling an ambulance.'

'I've just caught a chill,' I protested, not wanting to call the ambulance out for nothing.

The night before I had fallen asleep in the bath and by the time I woke up the water had grown cold. I had quickly topped it up from the hot tap, but I wondered if that was why I was feeling so ill: perhaps I had just caught a chill. I was also having trouble getting my breath but it was the hay-fever season, which had always affected me badly ever since I was a child. I was desperately trying to think of a hundred reasons why I might be feeling the way I was, avoiding the most obvious and the most frightening answer.

'It's just a chill,' I whispered feebly. 'Or hay fever.'

Alex refused to listen and made the 999 call. They were there within minutes and I managed to muster the strength to walk downstairs to the ambulance with a lot of help from the paramedics. I was itching all over, all the way down to the soles of my feet, and it felt like the itch was actually under my skin, making me want to tear it off in order to get to the source of the torture. Even the ambulance man noticed how violently I was scratching myself as we drove to the hospital. At the time I hadn't realised the itching was another sign that my kidneys had ceased to function, even though I can now remember that Mum used to complain about it all the time. It is an accepted side effect of kidney failure and now I have giant tablets that I chew ten minutes before eating, which help my veins not to calcify and control the itching. If the veins are allowed to calcify too far, I could just not wake up one morning.

The ambulance delivered me to the Royal Free Hospital in Hampstead and by the time we arrived the whole family was with me as we waited in Casualty for several hours. In the early hours of the morning, the nurses took me to an assessment ward and gave me some breakfast, which I immediately vomited back up, something which only really happens to me if I have food poisoning or something else specific. I shocked myself with the violence and suddenness of the reaction, beginning to believe that I truly must be ill. I was growing more and more frightened as I started to accept that this was not something that was just going to go away. I was approaching a point where I was going to have to face the truth.

Initially, the doctors couldn't find anything wrong with me and they discharged me later the next day, giving me one last straw of hope to cling to for a few more hours. I called Sheniece to come and collect me, trying to pretend to her that I was fine, wanting so much for that to be the case, even though I could barely stand.

When she got there, she found me sitting hunched over in pain.

'I'm going to find the doctor,' she said the moment she saw the state I was in.

I tried to protest but she had already marched off with a determined look on her face and returned a few minutes later with a doctor in tow.

She stood with her hands on her hips, looking down at

me. 'How can you release my mum,' she demanded to know, 'when she looks worse than when she came in?'

'We've tested her,' the doctor replied, looking at me a little doubtfully, 'and everything seems to be all right.'

'I think you may need to look again,' I murmured, 'because I don't think I even have the strength to get into the car.'

'OK,' he said. 'We'll give you a couple of days in the kidney ward, but I really don't think there is anything wrong with you.'

This was exactly what I had been afraid of. Was I wasting their time and taking up space that was needed for more seriously ill patients? Was I making a fuss about nothing when all I had was a chill? But at the same time I truly didn't think I could make it out to Sheniece's car without collapsing. I allowed them to put me to bed and immediately slipped into a deep and exhausted sleep.

The following day, I had a relapse that would almost certainly have killed me if I had been at home because the kids wouldn't have had a clue what they should have done to save me. One minute I was sitting up in bed talking to the whole family, who were all visiting, the next I started to feel like I was burning up inside.

'Alex,' I said, 'can you ask the nurse for some ice that I can suck? I really need to cool down inside.'

They brought the ice and I slipped a piece into my mouth, grateful for the coolness as it trickled down the back of my throat, and then I fell back on the pillows and into unconsciousness. The children were screaming for nurses and doctors, panicking, trying and failing to rouse me and certain that I was dying.

I drifted in and out of consciousness as the crash team was called and surrounded the bed with a lot of noise and shouting. Although I didn't know what was going on, and the kids tell me I was talking gibberish whenever I did come near to the surface, I remember clearly opening my eyes and seeing a crowd of strangers clustered around the bed, all looking concerned. By that time, the kids had been taken away to give the professionals more room to work.

They had seen me be ill before. All too often they had witnessed me slipping into my own world because of the diabetes. If my blood-sugar level goes wrong, I start to behave like a drunk, talking nonsense and falling about without realising it. There was one instance where I became completely unable to recognise any of them. I know that the scenes they describe are true because I can actually remember them after they are over, like waking from particularly vivid nightmares. I think it's a bit like being under the influence of powerful drugs, although I have never had any experience of that myself, never even having smoked a cigarette. I have never been able to see the sense in lining the pockets of the big tobacco companies or illegal drug dealers. I've always said that I would rather spend any money I have to spare on a burger from Wimpy or McDonald's than a packet of cigarettes. I know from my eating habits that I have an addictive nature, so I steer clear of anything that I think might be able to reel me into a habit that I then wouldn't be able to control.

I first became seriously diabetic in 1987, after giving birth to David, and tried to control the condition with diet alone to begin with. But I guess I gave in to temptation and ate naughty bits of chocolate or biscuits too often because since 1995 I have had to inject myself with insulin every day, usually putting the needles into my stomach, because my body has stopped producing the chemical naturally and I need it to counteract the sugar in my blood. To start with, I used to have to inject twice daily, but it has since come down to once a day. I'm so used to it now I actually prefer injecting myself all the time, if I have a choice, although sometimes the nurses on the dialysis ward insist on doing it themselves. I suppose they're worried that I will do it wrong and they'll get the blame for letting me.

If I get the blood-sugar level wrong and it falls too low, I will start to slur my words and talk gibberish, and the children know to find me some sugar quickly before I slip into a coma. If the sugar level is too high, I could slip straight into a coma without any warning. Once or twice the kids have panicked when they haven't been able to bring me round quickly enough and they have called an ambulance. The ambulance guys then give me adrenalin and sugar to get me going again, and sometimes they even put a saline drip up in the house. Aaron has become really good at spotting the signs, and whenever we go away on holiday he sleeps in the same room as me just in case something goes wrong with my breathing in the night.

In 2007, we went to Turkey on holiday with some neighbours. It was a long journey and I got off the plane without having eaten enough. I started to get ill in our room on the first day, drifting off into unconsciousness, and Aaron called the others, who fetched the hotel doctor. The doctor brought me back but the same thing happened again a few hours later. I realised then that travelling was going to become more and more difficult as my system became more vulnerable. My survival has become all about keeping a good balance at all times, which is hard to do on long journeys.

What was happening to me now, however, was obviously far more serious than anything the diabetes had done to me in the past. I lapsed back into unconsciousness again and the next time I surfaced, like a drowning woman bobbing back for the last time, I just had time to see that I was hooked up to machines before I slid away down into the darkness yet again. I didn't feel any fear because I didn't know what was happening. In fact, I felt quite peaceful, maybe because my body was preparing itself to die, or maybe because I was finally being forced to accept what was happening to me and I no longer had to keep up the pretence, not even to myself.

The next time I came back to consciousness, I was in another ward and I was told that it was my heart that was linked up to the machines. I didn't really understand what they were telling me, but I knew now that they were taking my problems very seriously indeed. They did the tests and they found that my blood was acidic and I was suffering from anaemia. The reason I couldn't breathe was that my lungs were shutting down. I was kept in that ward for three weeks, and when I did start to regain strength the doctors admitted that they had feared when I first collapsed that they had lost me.

They now knew for sure that my kidneys had given up completely and I was going to need regular dialysis if I was to stay alive. I had reached the dreaded stage five: kidney failure. It wouldn't be long before I would stop peeing for ever. If I wanted to continue living, I was going to have to spend a great many hours a week on a dialysis machine, and that situation would never change unless a donor could be found to give me a new kidney.

To begin with, they put a line into my groin, leaving it hanging there permanently, like some horrible fake willy, and I grew used to the idea that from now on my life was going to be reliant on a large, humming machine.

When the hospital discharged me, I had to make arrangements to go three times a week to the clinic at St Pancras, just behind the newly refurbished station, where the trains go whizzing back and forth to the continent. It seems ironic that I am trapped in a bed for hours on end, lying at Britain's latest gateway to the rest of the world.

CHAPTER TWENTY-ONE

STEVIE AND WHITNEY

Just because things sometimes go wrong, it doesn't mean that a large part of my life isn't still great. However ill I have become, I have never had to give up singing, and as long as I can sing I can continue to feel alive and happy and optimistic. Music really is the food of life, not just of love, and if you can combine it with good food as well you truly are in paradise.

Ciro's Pomodoro is an Italian restaurant in Beauchamp Place, just off Knightsbridge, where lots of celebrities go to eat when they are in London. Beauchamp Place is a fabulously smart little shopping street, the sort of area where Princess Diana often used to get papped when she slipped out of Kensington Palace for a bit of shopping or a meal with friends at the famous jet-set restaurant San Lorenzo. The Pomodoro is almost opposite San Lorenzo, and its southern-Italian owner, Ciro Orsini, is an ex-boxer and an ex-chef who has become a good friend through the years. One of the things Ciro is known for is his collection of photographs of the many celebrities he has met over the years in his capacity as a restaurateur as well as a businessman working in the film industry. In 2004, he even published a book of the pictures. He is one of the world's most colourful characters.

He often invites me to go over and sing with his house musicians when he knows there is going to be someone important in the restaurant, like someone from a royal family or a big-name model, a Hollywood star like Mickey Rourke or a pop star like Michael Bolton.

I met Ciro about 20 years ago when I was singing in another Italian restaurant and the owners told me about the Pomodoro and how lively it was. I decided to go and see for myself and I've been going back ever since. I usually take someone from the family with me when I go there to sing. Ciro lets us eat and drink as much as we like and then I get invited on to the stage to do a few numbers.

Ciro has become a close family friend. He even sent me, Dad and the kids over to Bahrain for Christmas one year when he was opening a restaurant there. In fact, Alex came up on stage with me there to sing, which was pretty much the first time she had sung in such a public place. She must have been about eight or nine years old. Dad had a great time too, never having been to the Middle East before. I think experiences like that make up for all the hard work and disappointments of life, but you can never predict where they are going to come from, or when.

Over the years, Ciro has opened branches of his restaurant in several glamorous destinations around the world, including Hollywood, but it is his Beauchamp Place flagship which is really the famous one and the one that endures while the others come and go depending on who he is in business with.

One day he called to say that he was expecting Stevie Wonder to come in later. 'Come over this evening,' he said, as casual as always. 'Maybe you can connect with Stevie. You can sing for him.'

I couldn't believe my ears. Me, sing for the legendary Stevie Wonder? Ciro must be mad. Why would Stevie want to hear me? The man is a hero in so many ways and for so many reasons. To start with, he is obviously one of the most talented singers, songwriters and musicians in the world, but he has also dealt with his blindness with incredible dignity and courage, never allowing the fact that he has a disability to stop him from doing whatever he wants in life. He is unquestionably one of the biggest stars in the world – one of the biggest stars ever really.

He first signed with Motown Records when he was just 11, after he was spotted singing on a street corner in Detroit, pretty much the same age that I was when I saw Lena Zavaroni and decided that I wanted to perform, and he is still one of the company's biggest names nearly 50 years later. His music has never gone out of fashion and he has never lost any of his popularity. That makes him one of the very few child stars ever to develop into a truly major adult performer. What makes him rarer still is the fact that to the outside world it seems like he is one of the few who has managed to make that transition without too much emotional damage. I've never met anyone who had a bad word to say about the man.

He has had something like 30 top-ten hits in America alone, including ten number ones, and most of his records have become worldwide standards, played and recognised and loved in almost every country on earth. He has won 22 Grammys, plus a Lifetime Achievement Award, which I think is more than any other artist, and he is able to play just about any instrument that has ever been invented. I challenge anyone not to be nervous and excited at the prospect of performing in front of someone as big as that, and, man, was I nervous that night.

Half of me expected to get there and find that he had cancelled or had to rush off early, but Ciro showed us to a table and I could actually see Stevie and his entourage laughing and joking on the other side of the restaurant while I was eating. Part of me wanted to go over and tell him just how great I thought he was, but I didn't have the nerve for that, and I didn't want to invade his privacy when he was enjoying himself with friends.

Eventually, the moment came when Ciro announced that I was there and asked me up on to the stage. As I walked up, my legs were trembling beneath me. I was about to perform in front of one of the greatest singer-songwriters in the world but I had to put that out of my mind if I wanted to hold on to my composure. I had decided to sing 'I Will Always Love You' again, as it had gone so well at the Stars in the Sky performance. It was a big risk because some of the notes are hard to reach, especially if your whole body is tight with nerves.

I have always felt a strong affinity with Whitney, ever since she first exploded on to the scene in 1985 when she was just 22, releasing *Whitney Houston*, which became the best-selling debut album by a female singer ever. From that debut, there was no stopping her. Her second album, *Whitney*, which followed two years later, was the first ever female album to go straight to number one. She had become one of the greatest stars in the world.

It seemed so great that a woman pretty much the same age as me could have such a huge success, even though I hadn't got much more than the tip of my toe on the show-business ladder by that stage myself. It helps to keep your own dream alive when you can see someone else, someone who you feel is very similar to you, achieving massive global success. But it can be frustrating too, feeling that another person has got there first, claiming for themselves the career that you were hoping was going to be yours.

Like me, Whitney had been singing ever since she was a child and was actually one of the backing singers, along with her mother, Cissy Houston, another Grammy-winning soul and gospel singer, on Chaka Khan's single 'I'm Every Woman', when she was just 15. Her big break came after she was spotted by Clive Davis of Arista Records (the same guy who had launched my beloved Bay City Rollers in America, as well as handling many other acts, including the great Aretha Franklin) singing in a New York nightclub with her mother.

Whitney's whole family is musical: Dionne and Dee Dee Warwick are her cousins and Aretha Franklin is her godmother. How awesome must it be to have women like that in your close family? I could imagine it all too clearly because of all the hours I spent round the piano with my grandmother.

I think Whitney and I have similar voices, not so much in tone, but in power. When I was young, I sometimes felt bad that she got there first and in my wildest fantasies I kidded myself that it could have been me up there on the screen with Kevin Costner in *The Bodyguard*, but I still think she's incredible. I would love to have had her career.

Despite the fact that she had a lot of personal problems in the late 1990s and was accused by the media of being involved with drugs, she still signed the biggest record deal in music history in 2001, when she was given $100 million to produce six albums. She even admitted to some of the drug accusations and in 2005 she would appear in a reality-TV show about her husband called *Being Bobby Brown*, which shocked everyone when they saw what bad shape she was in. I guess the show was trying to emulate the success of *The Osbournes*, but exposing that much of your private life to the world is a dangerous gamble for any star, however popular he or she might be. Just as reality television can make careers, it can break them too.

Whitney is divorced from Bobby Brown now and making a full-scale comeback. It broke my heart when I heard how badly things were going for her because not only had I followed her career from the start, but in 1999 I actually got to work with her. She had selected me from an agency I had joined to be one of her backing singers. I sang behind her on four songs, 'Learn from the Best', 'My Love Is Your Love' and 'It's Not Right But It's Okay', all of which appeared on *Top Of The Pops*, and 'Heartbreak

Hotel', which was never aired. It was a fantastic experience. Whitney was totally professional and friendly at the same time, with no signs of the prima donna-ish behaviour that I had been reading about in the tabloids.

Out of all the backing singers, she only spoke to me and even took a CD I had made, promising to listen to it. I have no idea if she ever did, but it was kind of her to show an interest when she didn't have to. I was in awe and a little shy around her and she lived up to all my expectations, especially when she sang live. *Top Of The Pops* had been notorious at one time for allowing acts to mime to their songs but Whitney sang them in three takes and did them perfectly each time. In a way, I was disappointed that she nailed them so quickly because I would have been happy to have stayed in that studio with her for ever. There was a definite air of respect around her and even the cameramen called her 'Miss Houston'. The one thing that really surprised me was that when she shook my hand her skin felt rough and brittle and I almost winced because I had been expecting her to have the soft hands of a wealthy woman. It was a nice little reminder that even superstars are human like the rest of us.

We recorded the four songs all at the same time and I got paid £250 plus some repeat money. When the Musicians' Union told me the payment had come in, I asked them to give it to the kidney ward in Great Ormond Street Children's Hospital. Mum had died because there weren't enough dialysis machines in the country and I wanted to make a contribution, however modest. I had wanted to find a charity that was specifically for West Indian kidney problems, but I couldn't find one. Little did I realise at the time that I would be one of the people to benefit eventually from increased numbers of machines in the hospitals. I guess it's true that what goes around comes around.

Now I was in the presence of another of the greatest stars on earth and I was actually singing a Whitney song to him.

I could see Stevie clearly from the stage and it looked as if he was listening intently, swaying from side to side, grinning happily like he does. The man has a talent for radiating joy from every pore. In a way, I was pleased that he was paying my performance so much polite attention, but it made me more nervous as well. His hearing must be so acute, his pitch so perfect, that he would be bound to hear even the most minor, insignificant out-of-tune note or wrong breath that I took. I imagined that something that a non-singer would never notice would be clearly audible to him.

Thank God for the hundreds of hours I had put in at festivals and clubs, restaurants and college gigs, for all the years of practice, because my voice held out and I gave an almost perfect rendition of the song, pulling the emotions of love and loss from somewhere deep inside me. So many singers are very young when they have their big hits, but I think often a song reverberates with more richness when it comes from someone who has lived long enough to experience all the emotions that the songwriters are talking about. A writer like Dolly Parton has certainly lived enough to be able to provide the raw material needed to touch the hearts of audiences when she pens lyrics like that, but it also helps if the singers of her songs have actually experienced the emotions she is writing about.

Ciro's diners roared their approval and shouted for me to do another song. I was nervous about looking like I was trying to steal the show from the house band, but the audience was insistent, so I sang 'I'm Every Woman'. When I'd finished this second song I resisted calls for more, stepping down from the stage feeling high on the excitement of knowing I had given two good performances.

When I got back to the table, one of Stevie's entourage came over and said the great man would like to meet me. Shaking with nerves all over again, I followed the guy to Stevie's table.

'Hi,' I greeted him nervously.

'Hi,' he replied with his trademark grin. 'Have a seat.'

As I sat, he clicked his fingers and one of the entourage handed him his Braille laptop.

'What's your name?' he asked.

'Melissa.'

'Melissa,' he said. 'Where in the USA are you from, Melissa?'

'USA? I'm not from the USA. My parents are from Jamaica. I'm Jamaican through and through!'

'Jamaican?' He looked surprised. 'I have never heard anyone from outside of the USA that sings like you. You have a world-class voice, Melissa. Will you stay around and come back on stage and sing with me later? I'd like to sing with you.'

'Oh my God!' I was like a gobsmacked little fan in his

presence. 'Are you serious? You wanna sing with me? Oh my God, this is not real!'

'Let me take your details, Melissa. What's your number?' He opened the laptop and proceeded to type in everything about me.

Later on that evening, he was called up on the stage and, true to his word, he asked for me to come up with him. Then Lennox Lewis, the boxer who was the undisputed heavyweight champion of the world, also came up on stage from his table to stand with us, a six-foot-six, 250lb giant of a man towering above us.

Lennox was one of the biggest sporting stars in the world at the time and a month later he would knock out Mike Tyson in a fight at the Pyramid Arena in Memphis, which was the highest-earning pay-per-view broadcast in history up to that time, generating more than $100 million. There had already been a huge amount of publicity after a fight broke out when the two boxers and their entourages announced the match to the press. Tyson had already served a prison sentence for assaulting a woman and had made headlines around the world when he bit off part of Evander Holyfield's ear during their contest in 1997.

Lennox is another lad who was born to Jamaican parents in the East End of London at about the same time as me, although he and his mother, Violet, moved to Canada when Lennox was 12. Over there he became an amateur boxer, representing the Canadians at the Olympics in Los Angeles and then in Seoul, where he won a gold medal. Boxing and singing, two of the traditional ways for black kids to escape from their backgrounds and get to the top in the white man's world. Lennox had moved back to England at the end of the 1980s, when he became a professional boxer.

The music started and Stevie sang the first verse of 'You Are the Sunshine of My Life', before handing the mic over to me. I didn't know all the words to the second verse, so I made them up as I went along, making Stevie laugh and clap his hands delightedly. Then we sang Whitney's 'Saving All My Love For You', a song which told of her love for a married man.

What a night! To be honest, I don't think life can get much better than duetting on stage with Stevie Wonder, while standing next to the heavyweight champion of the world. Such moments sure make a girl glad to be alive.

CHAPTER TWENTY-TWO

GOING TO CHURCH WITH STEVIE

At around nine o'clock on Sunday morning, four days after meeting Stevie at Ciro's, my home phone rang. I picked it up without really concentrating, still not completely awake.

'Hello,' a man's voice said.

It sounded like some oddball English toff. Since I don't know any English toffs, odd or otherwise, I was struggling to think who it could be.

'Good morning,' I replied, playing for time. 'Can I help you?'

'Yes. I wish to speak with Melissa.'

'This is Melissa. Who am I speaking to?'

'Steven.'

'Steven?'

I was getting irritated now. It sounded like someone messing around and I wasn't awake enough to be in the mood.

'Steven who? I don't know any Steven that sounds like

you. Forgive my lapse in memory but where did we meet? I don't recall your voice and I'm usually good at remembering voices.'

'I simply cannot accept that you don't recall our meeting,' the pompous voice continued. 'My goodness gracious me! We met at a restaurant and I complimented your astounding singing voice. It's utterly unbearable that you have totally forgotten our encounter. I had assumed that I had left a lasting impression upon you. It's obvious that I have made a grave error in judging your character...'

I couldn't believe what I was hearing. Surely I would remember meeting such a posh Steven. My God, they say that you suffer extensive memory loss when you are a diabetic, but this was ridiculous. I was beginning to think I should go back to the doctor for a check-up. The penny should have dropped, but it didn't, until the caller dissolved into fits of laughter.

'Hey, Melissa,' he said, sliding back into his familiar American accent, 'it's me, Stevie. Stevie Wonder!'

I had completely forgotten that he is known for being a wicked mimic and can do every accent under the sun convincingly. I was shocked into silence, trying to focus my brain. Was it really him, or someone winding me up? Why would he be ringing me at this hour in the morning? Why would he be ringing me at all? Nothing about it was making sense.

'Oh,' I said lamely. 'Hi.'

'Hey, listen,' he went on when we had finally stopped laughing, 'the real reason I've called is to ask if you would be kind enough to recommend a gospel church that I could attend this morning. And would you mind going with me?'

'Of course,' I said, hardly able to believe this was happening. 'Give me your number and I'll ring you right back.'

Singing next to him on stage had been one of the greatest moments of my life. Was I now being offered the chance to sing next to him in church? The whole thing seemed surreal but it wasn't an opportunity I was going to risk missing out on. I immediately set about finding the address of a great church I knew in Dalston, east London, while Stevie arranged a limo for us at his end.

'Get ready,' he said when I called back to tell him what I had arranged. 'I'll pick you up in an hour.'

Oh my God! In that hour I called everyone I knew. 'Stevie Wonder's coming round to my house! Stevie Wonder's coming round to my house!' I could hardly punch in the numbers quick enough my fingers were shaking so much.

I was yelling at Dad and the kids to put on their Sunday best at the same time as racing out the door to alert the neighbours to the fact that they were about to be visited by a superstar. I think they all believed I had finally lost my sanity, but exactly an hour later Stevie pulled up in a silver Mercedes stretch limo that took up nearly the whole street. The doors flew open and two bodyguards and his manager got out, all dressed up for Sunday service, plus an aide who led him from the car and up to meet my entire family, who were lined up like soldiers to greet him on his way into the house. The rest of the street had come out to stare in amazement, wondering how someone like me got to have one of the world's biggest music stars dropping in for tea.

Everyone was talking at once and Stevie seemed completely happy being at the centre of a whirlwind of people, all crammed into our little house, laughing and shaking hands with everyone until it was time for us to all pile downstairs again and into the limo under the gaze of all the curious onlookers. We purred out of the estate behind darkened windows like it was the most normal thing in the world to happen a few hundred yards from the gates of Pentonville Prison.

When we drew up at the church a little while later, I jumped out of the limo first in order to forewarn the ushers that they would need to clear a seat for him so he could get in easily and then get out quickly again at the end. The worst thing for any celebrity is to find that they are trapped with a crowd of fans between them and wherever it is that they want to get to, especially if, like Stevie, they are reliant on others to tell them where they are and which way to go. Things can get out of control very quickly and if anyone panics tempers can flare and fans can be left with the impression that the star is unfriendly, which isn't usually the case.

'Excuse me,' I said to the self-important-looking man on the door, 'I've got Stevie Wonder out in the car. He's about to come in. Can we make a space for him and his entourage?'

'Stop talking rubbish, sister,' he said, waving me away.

'No,' I said, 'I'm serious. Stevie Wonder is on his way in.'

'Girl, I ain't got time for this.'

By that time, Stevie and the entourage had followed me

up the steps and were coming in through the doors. The usher did a double-take over my shoulder and his jaw dropped as everyone rushed around to clear a pew while the rest of the congregation craned their necks round to see what all the disturbance was at the back of the church. The ushers found places for us and Stevie insisted that I shuffle in beside him.

More and more people were pouring into the church, word having spread, partly from my frantic phoning of friends earlier, until every seat was filled and people were standing all across the back. Everyone wanted to be part of this service, desperate to catch a glimpse of the great man, wanting to hear him singing hymns, hoping maybe to get a chance to shake him by the hand.

Stevie has very wide hands, so when the collection plate went past him I didn't notice what he was putting in until he passed it to me and I saw the pile of £50 notes sitting in a wrapper marked '£5,000' among the scattering of coins below. I had no money on me at all, so I had to pass the plate straight on to the usher waiting at the end of the row. Normally at that point the usher would move on and pass the plate to the next row, but when he saw how much was there he headed straight to the preacher, barely able to disguise his excitement and probably not wanting to take the risk of any of the notes disappearing before the end of the collection.

'Ladies and gentlemen,' the preacher intoned when the plate reached him, 'we are very blessed today. We have Mr Steven Wonder in the house.'

Stevie stood up so that everyone could see him, even

though he couldn't see them, waving good-naturedly around him.

'I'm so blessed to be here today,' he said, 'and I want to show my appreciation to God.'

They led him up to the pulpit so that he could address the whole church and he talked about how grateful he was to God for allowing him to come safely off the many plane flights that he had taken in his life. Then he sang a song praising God, with no backing music. Everyone fell silent and many of the congregation were crying at the beauty and sincerity of his voice. That is why some people become stars, because they have an ability to touch people's hearts with their sincerity wherever they go. Very few performers have managed to hold the love of so many people for as many years as Stevie has. Because of his music, I think we all feel like we have known him all our lives and nothing he has ever done or said has done anything to make us doubt his goodness or his talent.

Forty minutes later, at the end of the service, we walked back out to find what looked like the world's press clustered on the doorstep of the church, including the local radio station, all of them clamouring for the star's attention as he passed unexpectedly through their world, begging for a moment of his time before he disappeared back behind the darkened windows of the limo and was whisked away as quickly as he had arrived.

'Stevie,' a radio reporter with a mic shouted, 'can you sing us a jingle?'

Stevie just smiled and waved as we climbed back into the limo and headed home for another cup of tea.

Since then, we have stayed friends and he calls regularly to find out what's going on in our lives. Alex has sung down the line to him and he said nice things about her voice, just as he did about mine.

'She has an amazing ability to harmonise for someone so young,' he said, after listening to her demo. 'Did she lay down the voices on the tracks herself?'

'Yes, she did,' I said proudly.

'Someone should take her to see the CEO of Motown. Would you like me to present her music to him for you?'

I thought about it, but I decided that at 14 Alex was still too young to be catapulted so high up the music-business tree in one go. It's one thing to appear on a BBC talent show, or to sing live at some small or local venues; quite another to be picked up by the Motown global star-making machine, the one that created the likes of Diana Ross, Michael Jackson, Marvin Gaye, Martha Reeves, Gladys Knight, Smokey Robinson, Lionel Richie and Stevie himself. If that happened, her whole life would be taken over and she would be on the star-making treadmill with no chance of taking her time and looking around at the options.

Now she is older, of course, all that has changed and I hope one day she will be able to sing with Stevie, either on a record or on stage, just like I did on that magical night at Ciro's Pomodoro. An experience like that, which would once have seemed as much of an impossible dream as my announcing that I was going to appear on *Opportunity Knocks*, is now perfectly possible for her. Once the first door opens for someone in this business, all the others are suddenly within reach.

CHAPTER TWENTY-THREE

'MELISSA THE VOICE'

Ciro's has always been a lucky venue for me. On another occasion, I was singing there on a night when the Radio 1 DJ Bruno Brookes was eating at one of the tables with his wife. After I'd finished and had sat back down, he came over and introduced himself.

'You've got a terrific voice,' he said. 'I really like it. I'm doing the breakfast show on Radio 1 at the moment and I'm thinking of having a 15-minute slot where a singer comes in and sings live in the studio. Would you be interested in doing something like that?'

It sounded like a great opportunity to me and I immediately agreed. A few days later, at five o'clock in the morning, a BBC car arrived outside my front door to ferry me down to the West End. There's something about being professionally driven which always feels very luxurious, and being able to get somewhere without all the bother of working out routes and parking, and worrying how long it is likely to take you, makes for a much more pleasant experience. I can quite understand why wealthy people hire chauffeurs. Who would drive themselves if they didn't have to?

I was met at reception and escorted into the studio where Bruno was broadcasting to the nation's early risers. As I sat down, I was given some headphones, instantly making me part of the show.

'I don't know how this is going to go,' Bruno admitted while he played a record and the mics were off. 'Let's just play it by ear and see what comes in. I'm going to ask listeners to phone in with requests for you to sing.'

I pulled the headphones on, nervous that no one might call in but confident that I could handle whatever was thrown at me if they did. Bruno was making it all feel very comfortable and I was ready to enjoy myself.

'I've got "Melissa the Voice" in the studio with me,' he announced when the record came to an end. '"Miss MTV", and she is going to sing your requests live, so ring in now and tell her what you would like to hear.'

To our relief, the calls started to come in immediately. Mostly the callers were asking for classics and I would croon tunes like George Gershwin's 'Summertime' and 'You're Too Good to Be True', which has been done by everyone from Frankie Valli and Andy Williams to the Killers. The spot proved popular, particularly with truck drivers who were out on the road while most people were still tucked up in bed or having breakfast with their families, and the phone calls were stacking up.

The public reaction was so positive that Bruno and his producer decided to make a regular feature of it. It went on for weeks after that, with the car picking me up as dawn broke over the city and the calls coming in over the headphones. It seemed like great publicity for me and everyone at the BBC was being so nice to me I didn't think to ask for any money – again.

I never seemed to be able to make enough money to support us all. Life was a constant struggle for survival. People who only know what they read about show business in the tabloids, where journalists mainly talk about the wealth of the really big stars who write their own songs and earn from years of back catalogues, don't realise how hard it is for most acts to even make a living from their skills. There is the most enormous gap between the big stars and the rest of the business. If it was any other industry, there would probably be a revolution, but of course that will never happen in the music business because everyone at the bottom is imagining that one day they will get their big break and then they will be the ones sipping champagne in a Bel Air mansion. It's a bit like buying a lottery ticket, knowing that the chances of winning are virtually nil but wanting to try just the same because you also know that without a ticket you have no chance at all of winning.

The reality, of course, is that there are thousands of performers earning virtually nothing, even when they become fairly well known, because it is such an expensive business to be in with all the travel and the managers and agents and promotional expenses to be covered. We all keep on doing it because we love it, because performing in front of people who are appreciative is the greatest high possible. Most of us would still be doing it even if we had to pay for the privilege, which is sometimes pretty much what it feels like by the time you have dealt with all your overheads.

I worked as hard as I could at other jobs, some of them the most menial and depressing imaginable, but at times it just wasn't possible to make ends meet on my own. I can remember one day, when Alex was little, having to delve down the back of the chairs and sofa, hunting for the one- and two-pence coins that had fallen out of people's pockets in order to have some money to buy food. It was all the money I had in the world and I was too embarrassed to go down to the shop and have to count it all out on the counter in front of everyone. Alex was always the bravest of all of us and she took the coins and bought some bread and milk so that at least they all had something for breakfast the next day before going to school.

Despite the money and health troubles over the years, there have been so many good times too, and every so often I have been privileged enough to get a glimpse into the world of luxury that I guess most people dream about from time to time. Whether it is enjoying a meal in one of Ciro's restaurants or being chauffeur-driven to the BBC, these little treats liven up the daily grind.

After the Twin Towers were destroyed in 2001, no one wanted to fly anywhere for a while and so I was able to get some really good deals to visit Japan and Australia to see Angela and the others. I think it was £100 to Japan and £200 to Australia. On top of that, I managed to get upgraded to business class between Singapore and Sydney after something went wrong with the plane and we were delayed. I had to make a big scene and act the diva, but it was worth it, just to be given champagne in a proper glass, have my in-flight food served on proper china and to luxuriate amidst all that space and quiet instead of being crammed into the economy section as usual. Call me shallow but that moment I caught the bug for business class and from then on I wanted it wherever I went. Of course, I've never been able to afford it for a long-haul flight again, but occasionally I have treated myself on flights to Europe, just to get another taste of that other world, the world where folks like Whitney and Stevie and Simon Cowell live all the time.

CHAPTER TWENTY-FOUR

LIFE IS SHORT, SO MAKE IT SWEET

The hospital volunteers are bringing the trolley round the ward with all the snacks on display. I have got to resist. Oh my God, they've got Walnut Whips and I'm not even allowed to eat the nuts off the top because of my condition, let alone the cream and the chocolate. (I'm told that in Britain someone eats a Walnut Whip almost every two seconds and the manufacturers use up a million walnuts a week.) I mustn't think about it. I must hold out and let them go past. I'll look the other way, avoid catching the eyes of the smiling volunteers pushing the trolley and try not to think about it. Food used to be my best friend and now it is my deadly enemy, just waiting for a chance to poison me.

Even before I knew that my kidneys were packing up, my health was starting to become a major problem. I had no energy at all and I was falling asleep all the time. I remembered how terrible Mum had looked before she died, losing weight, her ankles and feet swelling like an elephant's, her hair falling out and those dark, dark circles under her sad old eyes, and I was terrified to think that the same might be going to happen to me.

Compared with Mum, Dad enjoyed robust health for most of his life and I never expected to lose him when I did. Many of his family lived to be over 100, and even when he was past 80 he still only looked about 50. Part of it was because he was so full of life and curiosity, always wanting to find out about everything, to talk to everyone who was willing to give some time to a garrulous old man. Angela was always brilliant at listening to him as he sipped on a Guinness and reminisced about his past adventures.

There had been a few health scares along the way, but nothing to make me think we were in danger of losing him any time soon. One Christmas at the end of the 1990s, for instance, he suffered a minor stroke while we were cooking the Christmas dinner together. A friend of mine sat with the kids for the day while I drove Dad to the hospital. He made a complete recovery from that, although we never did get to eat Christmas lunch that year. He only went to see a doctor about three other times in his life; once when he got pneumonia after living in my uncle's damp flat in New York, once when he got kidney stones and the final time, which was when the doctor had to tell him that he had lung cancer and that he hadn't got long to live.

Dad had been telling us he had chest and stomach pains for some time, but we had been thinking nothing of it, assuming it must be wind caused by his fondness for a regular drink.

Even before we heard about the cancer, I wanted him to

take a trip back to Jamaica with me and the kids to see all his relatives one last time and to explain to the kids who was who and where we had all come from. As usual, I had to save for ages until I had enough money for the tickets. Dad kept saying he didn't want to go, but I knew we would regret it if we didn't, so I lied and told him my sister was paying for it. He never argued with anything she said.

We flew out on New Year's Eve and he'd enjoyed quite a few drinks the night before, finishing up all the bottles we'd had in the house for Christmas. He actually went to bed in his clothes and got up to go to the airport in the morning without even shaving or washing, although he found the time for one more swift drink before rolling out of the house to the car. It was obvious he was still drunk when we reached the check-in desk and I got the kids to stand all round him, propping him up so the staff didn't see that he was swaying because I was frightened they wouldn't let him on the plane if they realised the state he was in.

'Just answer the woman at the desk "yes" or "no", whatever question she asks you,' I hissed to him as we edged towards the front of the queue. 'Don't go striking up a conversation or she'll know you're pissed and she won't let you on.'

He did as he was told and miraculously the check-in girl said nothing. We managed to get him on the plane without any more detours to any airport bars and he slept like a baby all the way there. From then on, the whole trip went brilliantly and the kids came away with a much better idea of where their roots lay and what their family's lives had been like before they left the island.

It was not long after we got back that Dad was given the news about the cancer, and he died seven months later. The kids were devastated because after David left their granddad was the nearest thing they had to a father. By just being there for them every day, letting them know that he could be relied upon and that he loved them, he played an enormous part in making them into the wonderful, well-grounded, secure people they are today. God knows how I would have coped on my own without his help.

His funeral was a real party. I was determined it wouldn't be a low-key affair like Mum's had been and I arranged for a horse-drawn carriage to carry him in his casket all the way from Holloway to the graveside in Enfield. When I went into the florist's to order the flowers, there was a documentary crew there filming for TV because the business was run by reformed criminals whose progress the programme was following. The director asked if they could bring their cameras to the funeral for some follow-up material.

'Of course,' I said, knowing that Dad would have loved to think his funeral was going to be on television.

When the carriage and funeral cars came to the door a few days later, with the beautiful black horses in all their plumes and finery, I was overcome by the same feeling of despair I had experienced when Mum had been lying in her coffin and I thank God that I had friends there to hold me and support me as I tried to cope with the overwhelming tidal wave of emotions that threatened to sweep me away. I couldn't stop myself from crying and shouting out my grief, trying to claw my way into the coffin to see him one last time. I didn't care who saw me or what they thought of me. I didn't even care that the cameras of the film crew I had met in the florist's were turning in the background, recording every detail of my misery.

'Oh my God,' I screamed over and over, 'he's dead! Oh my God, get my dad out of there!'

I was unable to imagine how I was going to be able to cope without him there. For all his faults and failings, he had always been my protector and my champion and my supporter, always there for me in his way, doing his best to help me cope with anything life threw at me, ever cheerful and optimistic. I don't think it matters how old you are when your second parent dies, it's always a shock, a terrible reminder of how little time we all have on earth to achieve the things we want to achieve. Most of the time I am very self-conscious about what people think of me, and I try my hardest to keep control of my emotions, but when I get to a pitch like that I lose all inhibitions and no longer care about anything, giving in completely to the turmoil raging inside me. I knew I looked like a mad woman, but all I could think about was Dad lying in the coffin and the fact that I would never be able to talk to him again.

The church was packed with three or four hundred people from the area, all of whom had known him over the previous years as 'Granddad'. He had liked nothing better than to talk to people in the street and the shops, especially the kids and especially when he'd had a few drinks and was feeling particularly in need of conversation. He was never good at holding his drink and sometimes, after just a beer or two, he would be talking to everyone and treating them all like they were his new best friends.

We buried him in his smartest brown suit and a Texan hat that I had brought him back from America in the 1980s and which he had worn almost every day since. In the church, we put a copy of the *Daily Mirror* under his arm, which had been his newspaper of choice for 40 or more years, and a packet of Werther's Originals, the old-fashioned butterscotch toffees that he loved so much, in his pocket. We were all crying and these tiny gestures of love even brought tears to the eyes of the undertakers, who you would imagine would be used to such scenes in their line of work.

For the church service, we were all wearing white and light colours rather than black, and at the graveside we let off seven doves, watching quietly as they fluttered prettily up into the sky alongside Dad's spirit. On the way back from the cemetery, the stress and the disruption to my eating habits got to me. I had an attack of diabetic 'hypo', adding even more drama to an already dramatic day, and had to be fed sweets bought from a petrol station to get my blood-sugar level back up so that I could get going again.

The gathering afterwards was everything a West Indian party should be, full of singing and dancing to calypso music while old men played dominoes in the corner, apparently oblivious to the noise and activity going on all around them. The revelry went on till one in the morning, with so much food the guests went home clutching doggy bags. My sister, who has a good job with the local council, kindly paid for everything and I hope one day soon to be able to pay her back, although she's always very nice about it and says there's no need.

It's wearing, always having to worry about money and where the next cheque is going to come from, to be counting every penny and constantly having to repay debts and favours from long-suffering and generous friends and family members. Sometimes it feels like it is never going to end, but throwing a huge party is a good way to forget all your problems for a few hours and celebrate just being alive.

CHAPTER TWENTY-FIVE

THE WINNER

Because Alex has competed on *The X Factor* twice, we have had a unique insight as a family into the workings of the modern celebrity-making machine, both the good and the not so good. It's an incredibly exciting experience despite all the downsides. There is always the problem of press intrusion, and the possible heartbreak of hearing your loved one being criticised in front of millions of people, or watching your child crying on screen and feeling helpless to do anything to soothe their troubles.

There is also the constant danger that someone will decide to make up and sell a story about you to the press. Exactly that happened to me after Alex won, when one of the newspapers rang me to say they had bought a story claiming that I was being investigated by the Benefits Agency for suspected fraud (I later discovered that someone had been paid £5,000 for supplying it to the paper) and asked me to comment. As far as I was concerned, there was no truth in it at all. If any government body has ever 'investigated' me, they certainly haven't informed me about it. It was annoying but I was determined not to let it get me down. I told them I had done five appearances for charity in December 2008 and that I had the receipts from the charities to prove it but they still ran the story. I even went so far as to show the receipts to the paper after the story had appeared, and they did print a retraction, but you would have needed a magnifying glass to spot it.

But the strange thing was that two good things came out of the incident. The first was that a new Facebook group was formed with the aim of finding me a donor, with two hundred members instantly signing up. And the second was that I received a number of emails from charities around the world asking me to help with their fundraising activities. One of them led to my doing a sell-out show at the famous Pizza on the Park venue in Knightsbridge with the band Soul Explosion. I didn't feel so good that night but did the whole show on adrenalin, before collapsing afterwards and having to be carried out of the venue, exhausted but happy.

There are advantages as well as disadvantages to having the media interested in what you are doing. In 2008, there was a report done into whether we should have an 'opt-out' system for organ donation rather than the current 'opt-in' one. That would mean that doctors would assume that a deceased patient was willing to donate organs unless they had registered as being unwilling to do so. There is such a shortage of organs and such a long queue of people wanting them that it seems like a good idea to me. I'm sure there are a lot of people who are willing to donate but just don't get round to carrying a donor card. When the announcement was made, I was asked by the NHS Blood and Transplant Service to do media interviews with all the major television and radio stations to give my side of the story as someone who desperately needed a donation. They even showed some live footage of me dialysing. That was how I bumped into Gordon Brown.

I had been invited on to *GMTV* to talk about why everyone needs to understand how vital it is that they agree to donate. When I came off camera, the Prime Minister was waiting to go on and came over to talk to me, which seemed to make all his bodyguards very nervous. They were watching my every move like hawks.

'I'm going to do everything I can for people in your position, Melissa,' he assured me. 'I am determined to get this bill through parliament so that this long wait for organs can become a thing of the past.'

I must still have been fresh in his mind as he went on camera because he very sweetly talked about me and about how brave I was for doing all the charity work I did, despite being ill, and that he hoped my personal suffering would be over soon. He even wrote me a letter afterwards. The NHS told me that the campaign had been a success and the donor register had increased as a result.

I wasn't that surprised when Louis Walsh sent Alex home from Boot Camp the first time because I didn't think she was quite ready to be a winner either. I knew she needed to get out and work some more hours in clubs and restaurants in front of live audiences, honing her skills and learning her craft. Three years later, I was damn sure she was ready.

'There may be other people in the contest who are as good as you,' I told her when she announced she was going to try again and asked what I thought. 'But I can guarantee you there won't be anyone with a better voice. Unless they've put in the years of graft that you've put in, and unless they've got a mother like me who can teach them everything she knows, they are not going to be better than you. You stand as good a chance of winning as anyone.'

Somehow we missed the deadline for the auditions for solo acts but I was determined that Alex should have another go, feeling sure that she was ready now and shouldn't miss the opportunity.

'Why don't we go together and audition as a group,' I suggested. 'They're bound to ask you to stay and not me.'

The plan worked perfectly and Alex was invited to go back on the show. I don't know what I would have done if they had actually let us on as a duo. I guess I would have had to admit that my health was not good enough and hope that Alex would be allowed to keep going as a solo act. As it was, it seemed that God was on our side.

When it was announced that Alex had qualified to go through to the live shows, all our neighbours threw a street party, decking the trees and houses with bunting, lights and balloons to welcome her back from Boot Camp, bringing out the barbeques and the music, creating an atmosphere just like I remembered from my parents' Saturday-night parties. I wished Dad could have been there to join in. He would have been the life and soul of the party, outrageously drunk after his first beer, telling anyone and everyone who would listen all about his wonderful granddaughter.

We kept on partying until the police came and shut us down for the night. Nearly all our neighbours have been living on the street for at least 15 years, most of us having moved into the houses at the same time, when they were first built, and we are a very close community. *The X Factor* results have to be a closely guarded secret for weeks after each of the recorded stages has happened, until the final contestants start appearing on live television, and we knew that we could trust all our friends not to let the secret out because they were all rooting for Alex to win.

When Alex was doing her interview with Dermot O'Leary during the audition process, I was hovering close by, listening in. Dermot's personal assistant, an Italian guy, was standing near me.

'See that girl being interviewed?' I said to him.

'Yeah,' he said, looking up from his clipboard. 'What about her?'

'That's your winner.'

He laughed dismissively. I guess they hear a lot of that sort of bravado from the tens of thousands of contestants and their families who troop through the audition process each year. The over-ambitious mother who believes her daughter is a future star is such a cliché in the world of talent shows.

'Don't laugh,' I said, my expression deadly serious. 'When she wins, I want you to find me and apologise for thinking I'm just another nutter.'

'All right.' He shrugged and wandered off, no doubt thinking that a nutter was exactly what I was.

The night that Alex won the final we were all backstage afterwards and I asked one of the crew where Dermot's assistant was.

'Oh, he's looking for you,' the guy said, 'he's over there.'

They brought him across and he had his eyes on the floor as he approached.

'Listen,' I scolded, like I was his mother, 'any time I tell you something from now on, you need to believe me.'

'Yes, Melissa,' he muttered like a naughty schoolboy accepting his telling-off.

'And now,' I went on, 'you and I are going to get married.'

I've never seen a man run so fast. I think we all deserve to have a turn at gloating now and then, as long as we remember that our good luck is never going to last for ever, that it is only on loan.

Throughout that year, I knew what thin ice I was skating on. I knew that I was lucky to have been allowed to live long enough to have seen my little girl enjoy such a triumph.

I was forced to miss one or two of the shows because I simply didn't have enough energy to make it to the recordings after being on the dialysis machine. My brain was telling me that the one thing I wanted to do was to be there to support Alex and cheer for her, but some weeks my body simply didn't have the strength to carry me there. Each week that I missed, Alex was kept in the running and I was given another chance to see her in action the following week as the ultimate prize drew nearer and the tension grew.

When I discovered that the final was going to be held at the Fountain Studios in Wembley Park in the afternoon after one of my dialysis sessions, I was determined to make it to be in the audience whatever happened.

I did the required four hours of dialysis in the morning, forcing myself to be patient as every second seemed to tick past at half speed and nothing could distract me from the horribly slow progress of the clock.

Finally, I was free and racing home. I tried to get a few hours' rest afterwards, as I normally would have done, but that day it wasn't possible. I was too excited and there was so much to do. An estate-agent friend of ours had sponsored us to print up some T-shirts with messages supporting Alexandra and they needed washing and drying so we could wear them again. A lot of our friends who had businesses had been keen to help in any way they could in order to be part of the excitement. Best of all, Angela had made a surprise trip back from Australia for the semi-final and the final, so we could all be together as a family again. It seemed especially appropriate since she had been living with us in the days when Alexandra first started putting on the shows around the house. You can actually see Angela swaying to the music of 'Hallelujah', alongside Sheniece and me, in some of the television footage of the show's climax.

Finally, I found myself in the audience, hardly able to breathe from the tension and excitement. If Alex walked away from this show as a winner, her whole life would change. It would be like the moment, all those years before, when Hughie Green's clapometer showed the world how much the audience had loved little Lena

Zavaroni, and my little girl would have a real chance of getting into the big time and leading a life unlike anything our family had ever known. I remembered watching Whitney at work in the *Top Of The Pops* studio and seeing all the respect that was paid to her. I remembered the reaction of the congregation in the church when Stevie stood up to sing. I remembered the feeling of standing on the stage at Wembley Stadium with the stars, singing to the whole world. I remembered sitting in the limousine with Stevie and in the radio station with Bruno Brookes and hearing my record on Mum's bedside radio for the first time. All those golden moments would pale in comparison with what might happen to Alex after today.

Even if she didn't win, I told myself, she would never forget this night's experience as long as she lived because she was going to be singing 'Listen' with Beyoncé.

Beyoncé is one of the world's biggest stars, but she is just seven years older than Alex. She also served her apprenticeship in singing and dancing contests as a child before joining Destiny's Child and selling 50 million or more records. She has also sold at least another 25 million as a solo artist. She then became a film star in *Dreamgirls*, which was a musical loosely based on the story of the Supremes and the early days of Diana Ross and Tamla Motown, earning herself two Golden Globe nominations and bringing full circle the story of the black female singing stars who have dominated the scene during my lifetime.

In 2004, Beyoncé won five Grammy awards. In 2009, *Forbes* magazine listed her fourth in a list of the 100 most powerful and influential celebrities in the world, third on its list of top-grossing musicians and top of its list of top-earning celebrities under 30, and now she was going to be holding hands and singing with my beautiful child.

Even after all these years, I still find it a thrill to attend a live show and then to go home afterwards and watch the recording at my leisure, better able to appreciate the details of each performance when the effects of the adrenalin have faded.

That night especially I needed to watch the recording over and over again because during the live show I was battered by so many emotions at the same time. The pride at Alex's fabulous performances, the tears when I saw how overwhelmed she was to be singing with one of her greatest heroes and the tension as we waited for the results. The relief when we heard she had won and the joy I felt at seeing her joy manifested so obviously in her hysterical reaction.

'Hallelujah', the Leonard Cohen song that Simon Cowell had chosen for the finalists to sing, and which would be the winner's first single, was such a stirring, powerful, moving piece of songwriting that it heightened all our emotions even further. It was like attending a great gospel service with a charismatic preacher whipping the congregation up into a fever, helped by the celestial sounds of a gospel choir.

The atmosphere in the audience is always great at these talent shows. We became good friends with many of the families of the other contestants and we continued to meet up at the live shows in *The X Factor Tour* that followed the final and everyone was so supportive of me as well as Alex. Most of the shows I could get to in a day, with a friend kindly driving eight of us back and forth in a rented van to places like Aberdeen, Glasgow, Birmingham, Cardiff and Manchester. When they were playing Belfast, I had to arrange to stay a couple of nights and have a session of dialysis while I was over there.

The night they appeared at the O2 Arena was my birthday and Alex gave me a shout out from the stage and the whole audience roared their approval. Every time I watched her, I felt the same surge of pride. People in the crowd used to recognise us as being her family and would ask for photos and autographs like we were stars too. At one venue, David and Aaron had to get a security guard to protect them from Alex's female fans.

At the O2 concert, Alex introduced me to Beyoncé backstage and we talked for about ten minutes, taking pictures.

'I've read about you and Alex on the net,' she said, 'and I loved the work you did with Soul II Soul.'

'Thanks.' It was such a kick to think that she even remembered. 'Can I sing with you after my transplant?'

She smiled and said yes!

She very sweetly emailed Alex a few days later and wished me luck with the dialysis.

The children's father started turning up to the live television shows as well but I tried to avoid bumping into him, knowing that I would find it impossible not to argue if we got into a conversation. I try my hardest to be forgiving about all the years that he left me on my own to bring up the kids, without ever offering to help out with the money or even contacting them at Christmas or on their birthdays. I know forgiveness would be the Christian thing to do, but I haven't yet managed it. Even the kids tell me that I should let go of the resentment now, assuring me that they are very happy with the way I brought them up with the help of my dad and friends like Angela, but I don't find it that easy. It would have been so great if we could have been together as a couple ever since the day of our hurried wedding in Jamaica, sharing the problems and the joys of bringing up our family, and being together when we watched Alex triumphing on stage. But that was one dream I was never going to be able to make come true.

Alex has been incredibly lucky, ending up as a winner of the biggest show on British television, with Simon Cowell's full backing for her future career. But still, nothing is quite as it appears to the millions of people who watch the shows and see all the sparkle and glitter, the tears and the hysterical audiences. Taking the talent-show and reality-TV path to fame and fortune is just as hard and fraught as any of the more traditional routes to the top.

From the music-hall acts that trod the boards in venues like the Hackney Empire to the performers who found levels of global fame previously unimagined in places like Hollywood and Nashville, through the pop stars who emerged on both sides of the Atlantic in the 1960s, the invention of the single and the album, the arrival of pop videos, MTV, iPods and giant stadium-rock tours, talent shows are just one more stepping stone between the obscurity that so many of us fear and the fulfilment of all our dreams of fame and fortune.

However they manage to win their first lucky breaks and bring themselves to the attention of the world, only the very strongest and most talented performers will ever manage to grasp and hold on to stardom and stop it from destroying them as it destroyed Lena Zavaroni and nearly destroyed Whitney and so many others.

Some people seem to imagine that, if someone in your family appears on television, all your personal and money problems are suddenly, magically, over. They are amazed to find you still have to shop in Lidl and Poundland. Other people think that, just because I was once a singer in a successful band, I have all the money I need stashed away in a bank somewhere. But I hardly made anything from my singing, and if anything it cost me money just getting to the gigs. I'm not complaining, because I don't want to be rich, but it would be nice to have enough money to be able to afford to live my life without having to worry and do calculations all the time when I am walking around the supermarket, terrified of facing the embarrassment of having to put things back at the till because I don't have enough coins in my purse. Likewise, I'm fed up with dreading every bill that comes through the letterbox.

But, as I lie in my hospital bed, listening to the hum of the dialysis machine, I know that in the end none of the money matters. Staying strong enough to enjoy the great moments in life is all that matters, living long enough to see your children grow up and prosper.

Like all families involved in competitions as big as *The X Factor*, with all its heightened emotions, we had our ups and downs along the way, many of which found their way into the newspapers with varying degrees of accuracy. All you can do as a parent is give your children as good a set of values as possible, tell them honestly how you feel and then hope that they make the right choices. All my children have gone on to make me proud of them in the way they have conducted themselves. One of my proudest moments during the whole run of the show was when I heard Simon praising Alex for the way she behaved behind the scenes. To me, that meant almost as much as when they heaped praise on her singing. It's hard for single mothers to stay on top of everything and it is often tempting to give up the struggle and just let the kids do whatever they want without saying anything, even when you know the path they are choosing isn't the right one.

Alex used the intervening years between her two attempts at *The X Factor* title wisely, taking every opportunity to sing in front of live audiences at weddings, in social clubs, pubs or nightclubs, building a following among the public who would be likely to show her loyalty when it came to voting time once more. She was 'serving her time' on the road in just the same way as entertainers have done since the days of strolling minstrels, polishing her skills so that she was ready when the big opportunity came along. It is my humble belief that she earned every one of the votes she received with the sweat of her brow and the strength of her determination.

To be able to watch your child fulfilling her greatest dreams in front of millions of people, to see how beautiful and radiant she looked and to hear how beautifully she sang was a privilege and an amazing emotional journey. Although I wasn't always able to get to every recording of *The X Factor* as I struggled with the illness, I fought as hard as I could to be there for her at the most emotional moments and I am so happy that I was allowed to live long enough to have such an experience.

When 'Hallelujah' was released, it became the fastest-selling download ever, as well as going to number one in the charts. All through this story, I have been talking about the great stars like Aretha Franklin, Diana Ross, Whitney Houston and Beyoncé and the extraordinary statistics of their sales and chart successes, and now Alex has joined their ranks and gone into the record books.

Now it's her little brother, Aaron, who is singing Michael Bublé and Will Young songs around the house all the time. He's not into rap and R&B at all, just like I wasn't into black music when I was his age. When he was tiny, he was a bit behind in his development and because he had never known his father I made a special effort to make sure he didn't go without anything. Maybe I indulged him too much. Anyway, he has always been a bit of a ladies' man and all the girls love him. He loves the whole show-business and celebrity thing, and is a great mimic, comedian and actor, as well as a singer. And hopefully the constant singing practice will pay off for him eventually, just like it has for his sister.

CHAPTER TWENTY-SIX

ONE DAY AT
A TIME

It's a great feeling when I look at the displays on the dialysis machine and see that there are only a few minutes left before I can be unplugged and released to get on with my life again for a couple of days.

It's like being set free, especially on the days when I'm feeling well and able to keep going without having to return home to bed. It seems like almost every day something happens to remind me how lucky I am to still be here.

It was a shock to hear that Michael Jackson had died: another casualty of fame and fortune, another child whose talent was obvious from the first moments he started to sing and dance, and a man for whom so many dreams came true but whose life seems to have often been more like a nightmare.

His music has been such an intrinsic part of my life. When I was about 15, Dad was given tickets to see the Jackson Five at the Rainbow. It was an exciting night for me, even though Mum insisted that we should leave the concert early to avoid the crush, which was undoubtedly sensible but disappointing for me when I just wanted to drink in every last magical second of the show before having to return to the real world. When we emerged into the night, there were hundreds of fans in the streets who hadn't been able to get tickets and who were milling around in the hope of something happening.

'Just as well we're getting out of here,' Mum said, taking me firmly by the hand and pulling me to safety, 'before there's a riot.' She was always nervous in crowds.

Three times I bought tickets to see Michael as a solo performer over the following years as he grew to be possibly the greatest showman in the world, and each time I fell pregnant and had to sell my ticket, not wanting to risk getting trampled in the crowd, my mother's warnings still ringing in my ears.

Some people thought Michael's televised memorial was tacky but I thought it was a great tribute. The world's biggest entertainer was dead and somehow it felt as if there was nobody else left to inspire the rest of us, even when I was listening to Stevie singing his tribute at the piano behind Michael's coffin. It was a horrible feeling, reminding me of how I felt when I knew that Mum and Dad were lying inside their caskets and it dawned on me that I was never going to be able to talk to them or see them again.

I staged a tribute night of my own at Ciro's Pomodoro with my friend Mannix, where we sang Michael's songs all night. I even made a hilarious attempt to do the moonwalk! At the end, I felt satisfied that I had paid my respects. It's sad when any part of the world's music dies and it's a reminder of how close we all are to the end and that it so often comes when we least expect it.

There have been so many times in my life when I should have died, or maybe never have been born at all. There must be a reason why I am still here against the odds, when so many other great people have gone. God must have a master plan of some sort for me. I can't wait to find out what it is.

EPILOGUE

I may have found a donor.

A family friend has stepped forward and tested himself. At the time of writing, everything looks favourable, but we still have a long way to go. There has to be further psychological evaluation and there have to be more health checks made before the hospital will agree to the transplant. But who knows? By the time you read this, my days on the dialysis machines may be behind me.